THE CHRISTIAN VIEW

OF THE

OLD TESTAMENT

BY

FREDERICK CARL EISELEN

Professor in Garrett Biblical Institute

NEW YORK: EATON & MAINS
CINCINNATI . JENNINGS & GRAHAM

CONTENTS

PREFACE

DURING the past half century the attitude of many men toward the Bible has undergone a decided change. The old confidence seems to be gone; a feeling of uncertainty and of unrest has taken its place. This small volume is intended to set forth the Christian view of the Old Testament, and to furnish answers to some of the questions men are asking concerning the Sacred Scriptures of the Hebrews, which the early Christians included in the canon of Christian sacred writings. The old foundations are not shaken. The Old Testament has stood the tests of the past, which have been severe and often merciless; and there is to-day stronger ground than ever for believing that in its pages "men spake from God, being moved by the Holy Spirit."

FREDERICK CARL EISELEN.

Evanston, Illinois.

7

CHAPTER I

THE NEW TESTAMENT VIEW OF THE OLD TESTAMENT

THE Christian Church has always assigned to the Bible a unique place in theology and life. What is true of the Bible as a whole is equally true of that part of the Bible which is known as the Old Testament. Indeed, until the middle of the second century of the Christian era, the only Scriptures accepted as authoritative were those of the Old Testament. Even then, only gradually and under the pressure of real need, different groups of Christian writings were added and received an authority equal to that of the older Scriptures. And though in the course of the centuries there have been some who denied to the Old Testament a rightful place in Christian thought and life, the Church as a whole has always upheld the judgment of the early Christians in making the Old Testament a part of the canon of Christian sacred writings.

It is worthy of note that the Old Testament played an important part in the religious life of Jesus. No one can study the records of his life without seeing that he gathered much of his spiritual nourishment from its pages. Even in the moments of severest temptation, greatest distress, and bitterest agony the words of these ancient writings were on his lips, and their consoling and inspiring messages in his heart and mind. This attitude of Jesus toward the ancient Hebrew Scriptures in itself explains the high estimate placed upon them by his followers. For, in the words of G. A. Smith, "That which was used by the Redeemer himself for the sustenance of his own soul can never pass out of the use of his redeemed. That from which he proved the divinity of his mission and the age-long preparation for his coming must always have a principal place in his Church's argument for him."(1)

The attitude of Jesus is reflected in his disciples and those who have given to us the New Testament books. Nearly three hundred quotations from the Old Testament are scattered throughout the Gospels and Epistles, and in a number of passages is the value of Old Testament study specifically emphasized. Perhaps nowhere is this done more clearly than in 2 Tim. 3. 15–17, in words written primarily of the Old Testament: "The sacred writings which are able to make thee wise unto salvation through faith which is in Christ Jesus. Every scripture inspired of God is also profitable for teaching, for reproof, for

correction, for instruction which is in righteousness: that the man of God may be complete,
furnished completely unto every good work."
Evidently the writer of these words considers
the sacred writings of the Hebrews able to inspire
a personal saving faith in Jesus, the Christ; to
furnish a knowledge of the things of God; and to
prepare for efficient service. And these are the
elements which enter into the life advocated and
illustrated by the Founder of Christianity.

An attempt will be made in this chapter to
determine the New Testament view of the Old
Testament for the purpose of discovering what
is the proper Christian view of that part of the
Bible. For, if the teaching, spirit, and example
of Jesus have a vital relation to Christian belief,
and if his immediate followers have preserved an
essentially accurate portrayal of him, then the
modern Christian view of the Old Testament
should be a reflection of the view of Jesus and
of those who, as a result of their intimate fellowship with him, were in a position to give a correct interpretation of him and his teaching.

We may inquire, in the first place, what is
the New Testament view of the purpose of the
Old Testament Scriptures? The answer to this
inquiry is furnished by the passage in the Second
Epistle to Timothy quoted above. Neither this
nor any other passage in the whole Bible warrants

the belief that the Old Testament ever was meant to teach physical science, or history, or philosophy, or psychology. Everywhere it is stated or clearly implied that the purpose of all biblical teaching is to make man morally and spiritually perfect, and to furnish him "unto every good work." Therefore we may expect that where the Old Testament writers touch upon questions of science and history they develop them only in so far as they serve this higher religious and ethical purpose. This being the biblical view of the purpose of the Scriptures, any theory of the Old Testament which makes no distinction between scientific and historical statements on the one hand, and religious and ethical statements on the other, is inadequate and erroneous, because it is not in accord with the New Testament teaching on that point.

The purpose of the Bible is intimately connected with its nature and character. The New Testament view of the nature and character of the Old Testament is suggested in Heb. 1. 1, 2: "God, having of old time spoken unto the fathers in the prophets by divers portions and in divers manners, hath at the end of these days spoken unto us in a Son." Four great truths concerning the Old Testament dispensation are definitely indicated in these words, with a fifth one implied: (1) *God* spoke; (2) God spoke in the prophets, that is, in or through *human agents;* (3) God spoke *in divers portions;* (4) God spoke *in divers manners;* (5) the words imply that *the Old Testament dispensation was incomplete;* it had to be supplemented and perfected by a revelation in and through a Son. The truths expressed here constitute the essential elements which enter into the New Testament view of the Old Testament.

The two expressions, "in divers portions" and "in divers manners," concern largely the external form of divine revelation. The former means that the revelations recorded in the Old Testament were not given at one time, through one channel or by one man, but at many times, through many channels, by many men, scattered over a period of many centuries, in places hundreds of miles apart. One result of this is seen in the fact that the Old Testament contains many books written by different authors in successive periods of Hebrew history.

The latter expression has to do with the different kinds of literature in the Old Testament, but it goes deeper than mere literary form. It means that in giving revelations of himself during the Old Testament period God used various methods and means, the different kinds of literature being simply the outgrowth of the various modes of revelation.

It is a universal Christian belief that God

reveals himself to-day in divers manners and modes. Every Christian believes, for example, that God reveals himself in the events of history, be it the history of individuals or of nations. Again, to many devout persons, God speaks very distinctly through the outward acts and ceremonies of worship. To thousands of earnest and sincere Christians connected with churches using an elaborate ritual, this ritual is no mere form; it is a means of blessing and grace through which God reveals himself to their souls. Moreover, God selects certain persons, especially well qualified to hear his voice; these he commissions as ambassadors to declare him and his will to the people. The belief in this method of revelation is the philosophical basis for the offices of the Christian preacher and the Christian religious teacher. Once more, in his attempt to reach the human heart God may dispense with all external means; he may and does reveal himself by working directly upon and in the mind and spirit of the individual.

These are some of the "manners" in which God reveals himself to his children to-day, and these are some of the means and manners in which God made himself known during the Old Testament dispensation. Then, as he does now, he revealed himself in nature, in the events of history, in the ritual, and by direct impressions; and at times he selected certain individuals to whom he might make himself known in all these various ways and who could transmit the various revelations to others. The Old Testament contains records and interpretations of these manifold revelations. It is self-evident that when attempts were made to record these various manifestations of God different kinds of literature must be used in order to express most vividly the truth or truths gathered from the divine revelations. The several kinds of literature, therefore, are the natural outgrowth of the manifold modes of divine revelation. In the Old Testament five kinds of literature may be distinguished: the prophetic, the wisdom, the devotional, the legal or priestly, and the historical. In their production four classes of religious workers who observed, interpreted, and mediated the divine revelations, were active: the prophets, the wise men, the priests (compare Jer. 18. 18), and the psalmists.

The prophetic literature owes its origin to prophetic activity. The prophets towered above their contemporaries in purity of character, strength of intellect, sincerity of purpose, intimacy of communion with God, and illumination by the divine Spirit. As a result of these qualifications they were able to understand truth hidden from the eyes and minds of those who did not live in the same intimate fellowship with Jehovah. Their high conceptions of the character of God enabled

them to appreciate the divine ideals of righteousness, and they sought with flaming enthusiasm to impress the truths burning in their
hearts upon their less enlightened contemporaries.
In carrying out this purpose they became states-
men, social reformers, and religious and ethical
teachers. No records have been preserved of the
utterances of the earliest prophets. But when,
with the general advance in culture, reading and
writing became more common, the prophets,
anxious to reach a wider circle, and to preserve
their messages for more willing ears, put their
utterances into writing, and to this new departure
we owe the sublime specimens of prophetic literature in the Old Testament.

In his direct appeal to heart and conscience
the ancient prophet resembles the modern preacher.
The wise man, like the prophet, sought to make
the divine will known to others, but in his method
he resembles, rather, the modern religious teacher.
His ultimate aim was to influence conduct and
life, but instead of appealing directly to the conscience he addressed himself primarily to the
mind through counsel and argument, hoping that
his appeal to the common sense of the listener
would make an impression, the effects of which
might be seen in transformed conduct. The
prophet would have said to the lazy man, "Thus
saith Jehovah, Go to work, thou indolent man."

Prov. 24. 30–34 may serve as an illustration of
the method of the wise man:

> I went by the field of the sluggard,
> And by the vineyard of the man void of understanding;
> And, lo, it was all grown over with thorns,
> The face thereof was covered with nettles,
> And the stone wall thereof was broken down
> Then I beheld, and considered well;
> I saw, and received instruction:
> Yet a little sleep, a little slumber,
> A little folding of the hands to sleep;
> So shall thy poverty come as a robber,
> And thy want as an armed man.

Nothing escaped the observation of these men,
and from beginning to end they emphasized the
important truth that religion and the daily life
are inseparable. From giving simple practical
precepts, the wise men rose to speculation, and
the books of Job and Ecclesiastes bear witness
that they busied themselves with no mean
problems.

Of profound significance is also the devotional
literature of the Old Testament. In a real sense
the entire Old Testament is a book of devotion.
It is the outgrowth of a spirit of intense devotion
to Jehovah, and it has helped in all ages to nurture
the devotional spirit of its readers. Here, however, the term "devotional" is used in the nar-
rower sense of those poetic compositions which
are primarily the expressions of the religious
experience or emotions of the authors, generated

and fostered by their intimate fellowship with
Jehovah. The chief representative of this literature is the book of Psalms, which is aptly
described by Johannes Arnd in these words:
"What the heart is in man, that is the Psalter in
the Bible." The Psalms contain in the form of
sacred lyrics the outpourings of devout souls—
prophets, priests, kings, wise men, and peasants
—who came into the very presence of God, held
communion with him, and were privileged to hear
the sweet sound of his voice. No other literary
compositions lift us into such atmosphere of
religious thought and emotion. Because these
lyrics reflect personal experiences they may still
be used to express emotions of joy, sorrow, hope,
fear, anticipation, etc., even by persons who live
on a higher spiritual plane than did the original
authors.

The legal literature differs from the other kinds
in that it does not form separate books, but is
embodied in other writings, principally in the
books of Exodus, Leviticus, Numbers, and Deuteronomy. All the representatives of Jehovah—
prophets, priests, wise men, and even psalmists
—were thought competent to make known the
law of Jehovah, but the Old Testament makes it
clear that at a comparatively early period the
giving of law came to be looked upon as the special
duty of the priests. These priests constituted a

very important class of religious workers among the ancient Hebrews. During the greater part of the national life their chief functions were the care of the sanctuary and the performance of ceremonial rites. But in addition to these duties they continued to administer the law of Jehovah, consisting not only of ceremonial regulations but also of moral and judicial precepts and directions. For centuries these laws may have been transmitted by word of mouth, or were only partially committed to writing, but when circumstances made it desirable to codify them and put them in writing the priests would be called upon to take this advance step. Thus, while it is quite probable that other representatives of Jehovah helped to formulate laws, the legal literature embodied in the Old Testament reached its final form under priestly influence.

The historical literature furnishes an interpretation of the movements of God in the events of history. It owes its origin in part to prophetic, in part to priestly, activity. The prophet was an ambassador of Jehovah appointed to make known the divine will concerning the past, the present, and the future. Of the present he spoke as a preacher; when his message concerned the future it took the form of prediction; but the case might arise that the people failed to understand the significance of events in their own history, and thus failed to appreciate the lessons which the events were intended to teach. If these lessons were not to be lost, some one must serve as an interpreter, and who would be better qualified to furnish the right interpretation than the prophet? This demand made of him, in a sense, an historian, not for the purpose of merely recording events but of interpreting them at the same time, and these prophetic interpretations are embodied in the historical literature originating with the prophets.

But not all Old Testament history comes from the prophets. As already indicated, the legal and ceremonial literature is due to priestly activity. Now, in connection with the recording of the laws, customs, institutions, and ceremonial requirements, the origin of these laws and customs became a matter of interest and importance. This interest, and the demand for information arising from it, led the priests also to become historians. And to these priestly writers we are indebted for not a small part of sacred history.

The third truth taught by the writer of the Epistle to the Hebrews is that God spoke unto the fathers in or by the prophets, which means, that he used *human agents* to mediate his revelations. The Old Testament may be more than a human production; nevertheless, it will be impossible to appreciate it adequately unless it is borne in mind that it contains a human element. In the first place may be noted the differences in style between various writers. These are frequently the outgrowth of differences in temperament and early training. Even the English reader can notice such differences between Amos and Hosea, or between Isaiah and Jeremiah. Evidently, whatever divine coöperation the biblical writers enjoyed, they retained enough of their human faculties and powers to make use of their own peculiar styles.

Again, the hand of man may be seen in the manner of literary composition. Most Bible students are familiar with the opening words of the Gospel of Luke: "Forasmuch as many have taken in hand to draw up a narrative concerning those matters which have been fulfilled among us, even as they delivered them unto us, who from the beginning were eyewitnesses and ministers of the word, it seemed good to me also, having traced the course of all things accurately from the first, to write unto thee in order, most excellent Theophilus; that thou mightest know the certainty concerning the things wherein thou wast instructed." Evidently, the evangelist carefully sifted the material at hand before he wrote the Gospel, just as a modern writer would do. In the Old Testament even clearer evidence is found

that the authors of the several books were guided
in the process of composition by the same principles
as writers of extra-biblical productions. The most
suggestive illustrations of this fact are found in
the books of Chronicles, in which reference is
made again and again to the sources from which
the compiler gathered his material. In 1 Chron.
29. 29, for example, mention is made of the
"words of Samuel the seer, . . . the words of Nathan
the prophet, and . . . the words of Gad the seer";
2 Chron. 9. 29 refers to "words of Nathan the
prophet, . . . the prophecy of Ahijah, . . . the visions
of Iddo the seer." These are only a few of the
references scattered throughout Chronicles, but
they are sufficient to show that in their composition methods employed by secular writers were
used. The same characteristic appears in the book
of Proverbs. According to its own testimony, it
contains several separate collections. After the
general title, "Proverbs of Solomon," in 1. 1,
the following additional headings are found: 10. 1,
"Proverbs of Solomon"; 22. 17, "The words of
the wise"; 24. 23, "These also are the sayings
of the wise"; 25. 1, "These also are the proverbs
of Solomon, which the men of Hezekiah, king
of Judah, copied out"; 30. 1, "The words of
Agur"; 31. 1, "The words of King Lemuel"; 31.
10–31 is an anonymous alphabetic acrostic. Similar more or less clearly marked phenomena may

be noted in other Old Testament books, all of them bearing witness to the presence of a human element in these writings.

More significant are the historical inaccuracies found here and there in the books. They may not be serious; the substantial accuracy of the writings may be established, but even the slightest inaccuracy constitutes a blemish which one would not expect in a work coming directly from an all-wise God. For example, 2 Kings 18. 10 states that Samaria was taken in the sixth year of Hezekiah, king of Judah; verse 13 contains the statement that in the fourteenth year of Hezekiah, Sennacherib, king of Assyria, came against Jerusalem. Now, the date of the capture of Samaria is definitely fixed by the Assyrian inscriptions. The city fell either in the closing days of B. C. 722, or the beginning of B. C. 721. Assuming that it was in 722, the fourteenth year of Hezekiah would be B. C. 714. But Sennacherib did not become king of Assyria until B. C. 705, while his attack upon Judah and Jerusalem was not undertaken until B. C. 701, hence there would seem to be an inaccuracy somewhere. Certainly, since the primary purpose of the writings is not historical, but religious, these inaccuracies do not affect the real value of the book. Nevertheless, their presence shows that the writings cannot be looked upon as coming in all their parts directly from

God. At some point man must have stepped in and left marks of his limitations.

More serious perhaps may appear the incompleteness and imperfection of the religious and ethical conceptions, especially in the older portions. Read, for example, the twenty-fourth chapter of Second Samuel. Jehovah is there represented as causing David to number the people, and when he carried out the command Jehovah was angry and sent a pestilence which destroyed, not David, but seventy thousand innocent men. Can any Christian believe that the God of love revealed by Jesus ever acted in such arbitrary manner? No! The trouble lies with the author of the passage, who, on account of his relatively low conception of the character of Jehovah, gave an erroneous interpretation of the events recorded. A later writer, who had a truer conception of the God of Israel, saw that a mistake had been made; therefore he introduced Satan as the one who caused the numbering (1 Chron. 21. 1). Or take the twenty-second chapter of First Kings, especially verses 19 to 23. Four hundred prophets of Jehovah urge Ahab to go up against Ramoth-gilead. On the advice of the king of Judah, Micaiah is called, who announces, after some hesitation, that the expedition will end disastrously. He then explains how it happened that the other prophets told a falsehood: "Therefore hear thou the word of Jehovah: I saw Jehovah sitting on his throne, and all the host of heaven standing by him on his right hand and on his left. And Jehovah said, Who shall entice Ahab, that he may go up and fall at Ramoth-gilead? And one said on this manner; and another said on that manner. And there came forth a spirit, and stood before Jehovah, and said, I will entice him. And Jehovah said unto him, Wherewith? And he said, I will go forth, and will be a lying spirit in the mouth of all his prophets. And he said, Thou shalt entice him, and shalt prevail also; go forth, and do so. *Now therefore, behold, Jehovah hath put a lying spirit in the mouth of all these thy prophets;* and Jehovah hath spoken evil concerning thee." Can any Christian believe that our God who is infinitely pure and holy ever did persuade anyone to tell a lie? God never changes; he has always been pure and holy; but man was not able in the beginning to comprehend him in his fullness. The human conceptions of the divine were imperfect and incomplete, and these imperfect conceptions are embodied in some of the Old Testament writings. True, as Bowne suggests, "God might conceivably have made man over all at once by fiat, but in that case it would have been a magical rather than a moral revelation."[2]

Throughout the entire book these and other

indications of the presence of a human element may be seen, which the reader cannot afford to overlook if he would estimate rightly the Old Testament Scriptures. But while they are there, they must not blind the eyes of the student to the fourth great truth expressed by the writer of the Epistle to the Hebrews, namely, that *God* spoke through these men; in other words, that there is also a divine element in the Old Testament. In the words of S. I. Curtis: "While it seems to me that we find abundant evidences of development in the Old Testament from very simple concrete representations of God to those which are profoundly spiritual, I am not able to account for this development on naturalistic principles. In it I see God at all times and everywhere coworking with human instruments until the fullness of time should come"[3]. The presence of this divine element was recognized by Jesus and by all the New Testament writers, and surely it is a significant fact that in the first outburst of Christian enthusiasm, and under the living impression of the unique personality of the Master, no doubt arose concerning the inspiration and permanent value of the Old Testament. With the Christian the testimony of Jesus and his disciples carries great weight. But without appealing to his authority every unbiased reader may convince himself of the nature and character of the Book; it is not necessary to depend upon the testimony of men who lived centuries ago, though they were inspired men. The Book is an open book, ready for examination, and inviting the closest scrutiny on the part of every reader.

Former generations found the principal arguments in favor of the belief in a divine element in the Old Testament in the presence of miracles in its records and in the fulfillment of prophecy. The present generation cannot depend upon these arguments exclusively. The whole question of miracles in the Old Testament has assumed a different aspect within recent years. In the first place, it is seen that in some places where formerly a miracle was thought to have been wrought natural causes may have played a prominent part, as, for example, in the crossing of the Red Sea and the Jordan. In other cases language which used to be interpreted literally is now seen to be poetic and imaginative. In still other cases the absolute historical accuracy of certain narratives has come to be questioned. All this has resulted in a weakening of the evidence relied upon by former generations. Approaching the subject of miracles from another side, a better acquaintance with the uniformity of nature and the laws of nature has led some to question even the possibility of miracles, while the greater emphasis upon the immanence of God has resulted in altered conceptions of the natural and supernatural, if not in an almost complete obliteration of any distinction between the two. Since miracles are involved in so much uncertainty, they do not at present constitute a very strong argument to prove the presence of a divine element in the Old Testament to one who is at all skeptically inclined; indeed, there are many sincere Christians who find miracles useless as an aid to faith.

In a similar manner, one cannot appeal with the same assurance as formerly to the fulfillment of prophecy. It is undoubtedly true that many prophetic utterances were fulfilled; it is equally true that some were not fulfilled. If, however, the apologist depends upon the fulfillment of prophecy as a proof, the nonfulfillment of even a single one weakens his position. Moreover, it is recognized at present that prophecy in the sense of prediction occupies a relatively insignificant place in the Old Testament. Besides, scientific methods of study have shown that some passages interpreted formerly as predictions can no longer be so interpreted, while in the case of others the interpretation is more or less doubtful. Here, again, the difficulties connected with the use of the argument have become so perplexing that many consider it wise not to use it at all. If used with caution, prophecy, especially Messianic prophecy, possesses great evidential value; but the argument from the fulfillment of prophecy as used formerly has lost much of its worth as a proof of inspiration. The arguments relied upon at the present time are simpler than those of the past, and are of such a nature that any fair-minded student can test them.

In the first place, attention may be called to the essential unity of the book. There are in the Old World great and magnificent cathedrals, some of which have been centuries in building, yet in all of them may be found unity and harmony. How is this to be explained? Although generation after generation of workmen have labored on the enterprise, back of all the efforts was a single plan, evolved in the mind of one man, which mind controlled all the succeeding generations of workmen. The result is unity and harmony. The Bible has been likened to a magnificent cathedral. The phenomenon to which reference has been made in connection with ancient cathedrals may be seen in the Bible as a whole, as also in the Old Testament considered separately. The latter contains thirty-nine books, by how many authors no one knows, scattered over a period of more than a thousand years, written, at least some of them, independently of one another, in places hundreds of miles apart. And yet there is one thought running through them all—the gradual unfolding of God's plan of redemption for the human race. There must be an explanation of this unity. Is it not natural to find it in the fact that one and the same divine spirit over-shadowed the many men who made contributions to the Book?

The proof of the presence of a divine element in the Old Testament which is derived from the essential unity of the book, is confirmed by the response of the soul to its message, and the effect which it produces in the lives of those who yield themselves to its teachings. Jesus and his disciples observed that its message rightly applied would awaken a response in the human heart; sometimes, indeed, it produced a sense of indignation, because it carried with it a sentence of condemnation; at other times it led to loving obedience. And they themselves experienced the effects of its teaching upon life and character: it was with truths proclaimed in the Old Testament that Jesus overcame temptation, and the quotations used in the darkest hours of his earthly life are an indication that at all times he found the most refreshing soul food in its pages. The same is true of the early disciples of Jesus. Undoubtedly, the statement in 2 Tim. 3. 15–17 is the expression of a living experience; and ever since these words were written millions of Christians have experienced the uplifting influence of many portions of the

Old Testament Scriptures. They may not enjoin the finer graces of Christianity, but they insist most strongly and persistently upon the fundamental virtues which go to make up a sturdy, noble, righteous, uncompromising character. A message which produces such divine results bears witness to itself that it embodies truth which in some sense proceeded from God. This is aptly stated by Coleridge in these words: "Need I say that I have met everywhere more or less copious sources of truth and power and purifying impulses, that I have found words for my inmost thoughts, songs for my joy, utterances for my hidden griefs, and pleadings for my shame and feebleness? In short, whatever finds me, bears witness for itself that it has proceeded from a Holy Spirit, even from the same Spirit which remaining in itself, yet regenerateth all other powers, and in all ages entering into holy souls, maketh them friends of God and prophets."[4]

As long as the Old Testament is able to awaken this response and produce these effects men will believe that it contains a divine element; and it will accomplish these things whenever men are willing to study it intelligently and devoutly. What the Old Testament calls for is not a defense but earnest and devout study. The words of Richard Rothe concerning the Bible as a whole are applicable also to the Old Testament Scriptures:

"Let the Bible go forth into Christendom as it is in itself, as a book like other books, without allowing any dogmatic theory to assign it to a reserved position in the ranks of books, let it accomplish of itself entirely through its own character and through that which each man can find in it for himself, and it will accomplish great things."(5)   The words of Professor Westphal are also worthy to be remembered: "The only thing for our more enlightened religion to bear in mind is that the proof of revelation is not necessarily to be found in the formula which claims to herald it, but, above all, in the specific value of the thing revealed, in the divine character of the inspired Word which forces our conscience to recognize in it the expression of God's will itself."(6)

The value and significance of the above argument cannot be overestimated. But during the past century other proofs have become available as a result of the careful, painstaking study of the Bible by scholars in many lands and from various points of view. These investigations have shown the Old Testament to be a peculiarly unique book when compared with other sacred literatures of antiquity. This uniqueness consists principally in the pure and lofty atmosphere which permeates the whole from beginning to end. One may read its stories of prehistoric times, its records of history, its law, its poetry, its prophecy, and everywhere he will find a religious tone and spirit which, if present at all, is much less marked in the similar literatures of other nations. The modern scientific student has approached the Old Testament chiefly from four directions, and in the pursuit of his work four distinct tests have been applied to the Old Testament: the tests of science, of criticism, of archæology, and of comparative religion. These four tests and their bearing upon the New Testament, or Christian, view of the Old Testament are considered in the succeeding pages.

Before closing this chapter one important question remains to be considered. It may be formulated in this wise: If there are limitations and imperfections in the Old Testament, or anywhere else in the Bible, how may they be distinguished from the truth? In the case of historical or scientific errors the method of procedure may appear clear to those who hold the New Testament view as to the purpose of the Old Testament writers; but the situation seems more troublesome in the case of religious and ethical imperfections, because religion and ethics are the rightful sphere of the biblical writings. If the Bible is not the final authority, where can be found a criterion by which the biblical, or Old Testament, statements may be judged? Startling as the suggestion to judge scriptures may seem in theory, a moment's thought will show that it is being done every day by practically every Christian who seeks spiritual nourishment in the Sacred Book. Who has not passed through experiences such as are suggested in these words of Marcus Dods?—"Who is at the reader's elbow as he peruses Exodus and Leviticus to tell him what is of permanent authority and what is for the Mosaic economy only? Who whispers as we read Genesis and Kings, 'This is exemplary; this is not'? Who sifts for us the speeches of Job, and enables us to treasure up as divine truth what he utters in one verse, while we reject the next as Satanic ravings? Who gives the preacher authority and accuracy of aim to pounce on a sound text in Ecclesiastes, while wisdom and folly toss and roll over one another in confusingly rapid and inextricable contortions? What enables the humblest Christian to come safely through the cursing Psalms and go straight to forgive his enemy? What tells us that we may eat things strangled, though the whole college of apostles deliberately and expressly prohibited such eating? Who assures us that we need not anoint the sick with oil, although in the New Testament we are explicitly commanded to do so? In a word, how is it that the simplest reader can be trusted with the Bible and can be left to find his own spiritual nourishment in it, rejecting almost as much as he receives?"(⁷) These questions call attention to a common Christian practice. But, if the practice can be justified as Christian, the principle underlying the practice may be Christian also; and so it is, for it is recognized as legitimate in the New Testament.

A single sentence from a New Testament book suggests the answer to the above questions: "He that is spiritual judgeth all things."(⁸) The Scriptures are included among the "all things." But notice, Paul does not say that anyone may set himself up as judge, but "he that is spiritual"; that is, the man who is controlled by the spirit of the Christ. If Jesus has given to the world the highest revelation of God and truth, then the expressions of all other revelations must be measured by his revelation, either as an external standard, or as an inner criterion by him who, in his own experience, has appropriated the character, spirit, and life of Jesus. He who has thus appropriated the Christ in his fullness will be able to judge all things. But until he has reached that standard man's judgment will remain imperfect and more or less unreliable, and though for his own guidance he is still dependent upon it, he must guard against the error of setting up his own imperfect Christian consciousness as the ultimate criterion for all.

Up to the present time no individual has reached the stage of experience where he may be appealed to as final authority for all. Perhaps the sum total of the general Christian consciousness would prove a more reliable guide, or the Church in so far as it embodies this consciousness. But it also still falls short of its final glory. It is in the process of development toward perfection, but it has not yet reached that stage, and will not reach it until the consciousness of every individual contributing to it reflects the consciousness of Jesus himself. Then, and then only, can it be appealed to as an ultimate criterion in matters religious or Christian, including the specific question under consideration: What in the Old Testament is from God, and so, permanent, and what is due to the human limitations of the authors, and so, temporary and local?

It seems, therefore, necessary to appeal at the present time to what may be called, in a sense, an external standard: the spirit, the teaching, and the life of Jesus as it may be determined objectively from the gospel records. The supreme position occupied by Jesus the Christ in Christian thinking is well described by W. N. Clarke: "He [Jesus Christ] has shown God as he is in his character and relations with men. He has represented life in its true meaning, and opened to us the real way to genuine welfare and success in existence.

What he has made known commends and proves itself as true by the manner in which it fits into the human scheme, meets human needs, and renders thought rational and life successful. God eternally is such a being as Jesus represents him to be—this is the heart of Christianity, to be apprehended, not first in thought but first in life and love, and this is forever true. And it is a revelation never to be superseded, but forever to be better and better known."([9]) By this standard, called by Clarke the Christian element in the Bible, the Old Testament teaching must be measured; and by the application of this standard alone is it possible to separate the human from the divine and to estimate rightly the permanent value of Old or New Testament teaching. Whatever in the Scriptures endures this test may be received as of permanent religious value, because it is divine in the deepest sense.

NOTES ON CHAPTER I

([1]) Modern Criticism and the Preaching of the Old Testament, p. 19.

([2]) Studies in Christianity, p. 73.

([3]) Primitive Semitic Religions To-day, p. 14.

([4]) Letters on the Inspiration of the Scriptures, Letter I.

([5]) Quoted in the Old Testament Student, Vol. VIII, p. 84.

([6]) The Law and the Prophets, p. 16.

([7]) The Bible, Its Origin and Nature, pp. 160, 161.

([8]) 1 Cor. 2. 15.

([9]) The Use of the Scriptures in Theology, pp. 51, 52.

CHAPTER II

THE OLD TESTAMENT AND MODERN SCIENCE

FOR many centuries during the Christian era
science was almost completely dominated by
theology. Whenever, therefore, a scientific investigator proposed views not in accord with the
theological notions of the age he was considered
a heretic and condemned as such. During these
same centuries theology was dominated by a
view of the Bible which valued the latter as an
infallible authority in every realm of human
thought. The view of the Bible held then was
expressed as late as 1861 in these words: "The
Bible is none other than the voice of Him that
sitteth upon the throne. Every book of it, every
chapter of it, every verse of it, every word of it,
every syllable of it (where are we to stop?), every
letter of it, is the direct utterance of the Most
High. The Bible is none other than the word of
God; not some part of it more, some part of it
less, but all alike, the utterance of Him who sitteth
upon the throne, faultless, unerring, supreme."(1)
A book which came thus directly from the mind
of God must be inerrant and infallible; hence
closely associated with this mechanical view of

the divine origin of the Bible was the belief in its absolute inerrancy and infallibility. This is clearly recognized in the words of two eminent American theologians: "The historical faith of the Church has always been that the affirmations of the scriptures of all kinds, whether of spiritual doctrine or duty, or of physical or historical fact, or of psychological or philosophical principle, are without any error, when the *ipsissima verba* of the autographs are ascertained and interpreted in their natural and intended sense."[2]

With such an estimate of the Bible it is only natural that theology should bitterly resent any and all scientific conclusions which seemed to be contrary to the statements of the Bible. However, a study of the history of Bible interpretation creates a serious perplexity. The principles upon which the interpretations rested were not the same in all ages. As a result, the "natural and intended sense" of biblical statements was variously apprehended. What was considered the clear teaching of Scripture in one age might be condemned as unscriptural in another. Moreover, some of the methods of interpretation are not calculated to inspire confidence in the results. When, for example, the poetic passage,

> Sun, stand thou still upon Gibeon,
> And thou, moon, in the valley of Aijalon.
> And the sun stood still, and the moon stayed, [3]

is considered sufficient to discredit the scientific claim that the earth moves around the sun, rather than the sun around the earth, one's confidence in the truth of the theological view is somewhat shaken. It may be insisted, then, that much of the so-called conflict between science and the Bible was in reality a conflict between science and a misinterpreted Bible.

This, even theology seems to have recognized, for again and again it changed its interpretation of the Bible so as to bring it into accord with the persistent claims of science. "The history of most modern sciences," says Farrar, "has been as follows: their discoverers have been proscribed, anathematized, and, in every possible instance, silenced or persecuted; yet before a generation has passed the champions of a spurious orthodoxy have had to confess that their interpretations were erroneous; and—for the most part without an apology and without a blush—have complacently invented some new line of exposition by which the phrases of Scripture can be squared into semblable accordance with the now acknowledged fact."(4)

The so-called historical method of Bible study, which has gradually won its way, at least in Protestant Christianity, has established Bible interpretation upon a firmer foundation, so that at present much less uncertainty exists as to the meaning of the Bible than at any preceding age. In the same way scientific investigation has made remarkable strides during the nineteenth century; Twentieth century science is far different from that of the early years of the preceding century. And as scientists have had to surrender many of their positions in the past it is very probable that, as the result of further investigation, some views held at present will be superseded by others. Nevertheless, though science cannot as yet dispense with working hypotheses which may or may not prove true, and though modifications in certain widely accepted views may be expected, there are many conclusions which may be considered firmly established. This being the case, if at the present time the conflict between science and the Bible is discussed, it is a conflict between scientific conclusions reached after prolonged, careful study and investigation and the teaching of the Bible as determined by the scientific use of all legitimate means of interpretation.

Does such conflict exist? Many geologists, astronomers, biologists, and other scientists have claimed for some time that they have reached conclusions not in accord with certain statements of the Bible. Take as an illustration the biblical and scientific statements concerning the age of the earth, or creation in general.([5]) The general conclusion reached by an overwhelming majority

of the most competent students of the Bible has
been that according to the information furnished
by the Scriptures, the date of creation was, in
round numbers, four thousand years before the
opening of the Christian era.([6]) At that time,
in the words of the Westminster Confession,([7])
"It pleased God . . . to create or make of nothing
the world and all things therein whether visible
or invisible in the space of six days and all very
good." This was accepted as the plain teaching
of the first chapter of Genesis even after scientific
methods had been introduced in the study of
the Bible. Then came geology, pushing back the
"beginnings," adding millions of years to the age
of the globe, and insisting that there is abundant
evidence to prove the existence of life upon earth
many millenniums before B. C. 4,000. Other
sciences reached conclusions pointing in the same
direction, until it became perfectly evident that
Bible students must reckon with what seemed a
real conflict between the conclusions of science and
the teaching of the Bible.

No wonder Bible lovers were troubled when
scientists in ever-increasing numbers advanced
claims that appeared to involve a charge of
scientific inaccuracy against the Sacred Scriptures.
Many were convinced that this could not be,
for they feared that if the Bible contained inaccuracies of any sort, its value would be com-

pletely destroyed, and with the Bible Christianity
must fall into ruins. In Brother Anthony, intended to picture the perplexed soul of a monk
in the days of Galileo, Mark Guy Pearse gives a
vivid portrayal of the doubts and perplexities of
many devout Bible students in the nineteenth
century:

> But on my fevered heart there falls no balm;
> The garden of my soul, where happy birds
> Sang in the fullness of their joy, and bloomed
> The flowers bright, finds only winter now;
> And bleak winds moan about the leafless trees,
> And chill rains beat to earth the rotting stalks.
> Hope, Faith, and God, alike are gone, all gone—
> If it be so, as this Galileo saith.
> *"The earth is round and moves about the sun;*
> *The sun," he saith, "is still, the axle fixed*
> *Of nature's wheel, center of all the worlds."*
> Galileo is an honest soul, God knows—
> No end has he to serve but only truth,
> By that which he declares, daring to risk
> Position, liberty, and even life itself. He knows.
> And yet the ages have believed it not.
> Have they not meditated, watched, and prayed—
> Great souls with vision purged and purified?
> Had God no messenger until arose
> Galileo! Long years the Church has prayed,
> Seeking His grace who guided into truth,
> And weary eyes have watched the sun and stars,
> And heard the many voices that proclaim
> God's hidden ways—did they believe a lie?
> The Church's holy fathers, were they wrong?
> Yet speaks Galileo as one who knows.
>
> Shrinks all my soul from breathing any word
> That dares to question God's most holy Book,

As men beneath an avalanche pass dumb
For fear a sound should bring destruction down.
If but a jot or tittle of the Word
Do pass away, then is all lost. And yet
If what Galileo maintains be true!—
"The sun itself moves not." The Scripture tells
At Joshua's command the sun stood still.
Doth scripture lie? The blessed Lord himself,
Spake he not of the sun that rose and set!
So cracks and cleaves the ground beneath my feet.

The sun that fills and floods the world with light
My darkness and confusion hath become!
O God, as here about the old gray walls
The ivy clings and twines its arms, and finds
A strength by which it rises from the earth
And mounts toward heaven, then gladly flings
Its grateful crown of greenery round the height,
So by thy Word my all uncertain soul
Hath mounted toward thy heaven, and brought
Its love, its all, wherewith to crown my Lord.
Alas, the wall is fallen. Beneath it crushed
The clinging ivy lies; its stronghold once
Is now the prison house, the cruel grave.[8]

Since the scientific position seemed to many
devout believers to undermine the Christian faith,
it is not altogether strange that they should set
themselves against these claims with all their
might, though it may be difficult to justify the
bitterness displayed by many Christian ministers
in the denunciation of even devout Christian
scientists, as "infidels," "impugners of the sacred
records," "assailants of the Word of God," etc.
It is hardly credible that during the enlightened

nineteenth century geology should be denounced as "not a subject of lawful inquiry," "a dark art," "dangerous and disreputable," "a forbidden province," "infernal artillery," "an awful evasion of the testimony of revelation."

But the progress of science could not be blocked by denunciation, and gradually the claims of geology, astronomy, and other sciences respecting the great age of the earth came to be accepted as well established. Is, then, the scientific teaching of the Bible false? By no means, said many defenders of the faith; on the contrary, there is perfect agreement between science and the Bible, provided the latter is rightly interpreted. The first problem was to extend what was commonly taken to be the biblical teaching respecting the age of the earth so as to meet the demands of geology. This was readily done by interpreting "day" figuratively as meaning an indefinite period. It could easily be shown that in some passages "day" did not mean a day of twenty-four hours. Hence, why not interpret the word metaphorically in Gen. 1? It is safe to say that, had it not been for a desire to harmonize the biblical account with the conclusions of science, no Bible student would ever have thought of this interpretation in connection with the acts of creation, for a natural interpretation of the writer's language makes it evident that when the author of Gen. 1 speaks of the successive events of creation he is thinking of days of twenty-four hours, each consisting of day and night.([9]) Marcus Dods is right when he says, "If the word 'day' in these chapters does not mean a period of twenty-four hours, the interpretation of scripture is hopeless."([10]) No permanent good can come from doing violence to plain statements of the Bible by the use of methods of interpretation that would be considered illegitimate in the study of other literary productions. In all the harmonizing efforts this caution has been overlooked. The believer in revelation, thinking that the agreement between science and the Bible must be minute, has yielded to the temptation to twist the biblical record into a new meaning with every fresh discovery of science. Many scientists were repelled by this arbitrary method, and when they saw that agreement could not be had by legitimate methods, and knew of no other way out of the difficulty, they too frequently assumed a hostile attitude toward revelation. A method leading to such disastrous results cannot be considered altogether satisfactory.

Granting, however, for the sake of argument, the possibility of interpreting "day" metaphorically, the troubles are by no means ended, for it is impossible to discover clearly defined periods in the geological records such as are presupposed in the biblical record. But there is a more serious difficulty. The order in which the different living beings and the heavenly bodies are said in Genesis to have been created does not seem to be the same as that suggested by geology and astronomy. For example, according to Genesis, fishes and birds appeared together on the fifth day, preceding all land animals, which are said to have been created on the sixth day. According to geology, fish and numerous species of land animals, especially reptiles living on land, preceded birds.([11]) Moreover, according to Genesis, the sun, moon, and stars were created after the earth, a view which is altogether inconsistent with the modern scientific view of the universe, and of the part the sun plays in plant and animal life upon earth. True, this last difficulty is avoided by some by giving to certain Hebrew words a meaning which they do not ordinarily have. For example, it is said, "Let there be" (verse 14) means "Let there appear"; "God made" (verse 16) means "God made to appear," or "God appointed," to a specific office. With this interpretation, it is stated, Genesis says nothing about the formation or creation of the luminaries. They may have existed for a long time, only on the fourth day they were made to appear—the vapor around the earth having previously hidden them—and were appointed to the offices mentioned in verses 14 to 18. No one will claim that this is a natural

interpretation of the biblical language. If the
writer meant "Let there appear," he could have
found a suitable word in Hebrew, as also to express
the idea "appoint." The language of Driver is
not too strong: "Verses fourteen to eighteen cannot
be legitimately interpreted except as implying that
in the conception of the writer luminaries had not
previously existed, and that they were made and
set in their places in the heavens after the separation of sea and land and the appearance of vegetation upon the earth."([12])

Various attempts have been made to escape the
difficulty caused by the conclusions of geology as
to the order in which different forms of life have
appeared upon earth. These conclusions are based
chiefly upon the presence of fossil remains im-
bedded in the different strata of the earth's
surface. Passing by the earlier explanations—for
example, that these fossil remains were placed
there by a direct act of God on one of the creative
days for some mysterious purpose, perhaps for the
trial of human faith, or that they were due to
the ravages of the Deluge—reference may be made
to two or three of the more recent "scientific"
attempts to harmonize the facts of science with
the statements of Genesis. There is, first of all,
the *restitution* theory advocated by J. H. Kurtz
and Thomas Chalmers.([13]) Admitting that the
fossil remains are important for the determination

of the age of the earth and the order in which
different forms of life appeared upon the globe,
Kurtz writes: "The animal and vegetable world
which lies buried in the stratified formations was
not that which, according to the Bible, was
created respectively on the third, fifth, and
sixth days. Its origin must belong to an earlier
period."([14]) In other words, his view is that "the
main description in Genesis does not relate to
the geological periods at all; that room is left for
these periods between verse one and verse two;
that the life which then flourished upon the
earth was brought to an end by a catastrophe,
the results of which are alluded to in verse two;
and that what follows (verses 3ff.) is the description of a second creation immediately preceding
the appearance of man." That this view is due
to a desire to harmonize the biblical account
with science is clearly implied in the words of
Kurtz intended to meet the charge of Delitzsch
that his view is "pure delusion." "It is," says
Kurtz, "merely a delusion to attempt identifying
the creation of the primeval fossil flora and fauna
with those of the third, fifth, and sixth days,
*and at the same time to endeavor harmonizing
geology and the Bible*." Not to speak of the
astronomical difficulty referred to above, which
remains, science has nothing whatever to offer
in support of this theory, while, on the other

hand, the tenor of the Genesis narrative implies such close connection between verse one and verse two that there is no room for the alleged catastrophe. It is not strange, therefore, that modern apologists have discarded the restitution hypothesis.

The *vision* theory has been presented most forcefully by Hugh Miller.([15]) According to this view "the narrative was not meant to describe the actual succession of events, but was the description of a series of visions presented prophetically to the narrator's mental eye, and representing, not the first appearance of each species of life upon the globe, but its maximum development. The 'drama of creation,' it is said, is not described as it was enacted historically, but *optically*, as it would present itself to a spectator in a series of pictures or tableaux embodying the most characteristic and conspicuous feature of each period, and, as it were, summarizing in miniature its results."

Though this view was presented with much eloquence and skill, it has been unable to maintain its position, simply because it is based upon an unnatural interpretation of the biblical record. No one approaching Genesis without a theory to defend would think for a moment that he is reading the description of a vision. The only natural interpretation is that the author means to record what he considers actual fact. Moreover, where in Scripture could there be found an analogy to this mode of procedure? The revelation of an unknown past to a historian or prophet seems not in accord with the ordinary method of God's revelations to men. But, admitting the possibility of this method of divine communication, why should the picture thus presented to the mind of the author differ so widely from the facts uncovered by geologists?

Similar attempts to harmonize Genesis with theology have been made by other geologists, among them Professor Alexander Winchell,([16]) Sir J. W. Dawson,([17]) and Professor J. D. Dana.([18]) The results are perfectly satisfactory to these writers, but they fail to see that in order to accomplish their purpose they must have recourse to unnatural interpretations of the Genesis account, which in itself is sufficient evidence to show the hopelessness of the task. A similar judgment must be passed on the more recent attempt by F. H. Capron([19]) to bring the biblical account into harmony with the modern theory of evolution. Capron is fully convinced that "the most rudimentary knowledge of geology is sufficient to satisfy any candid critic that the Genesis narrative as interpreted by any one of them([20]) cannot be brought into harmony with the admitted facts of science." He, therefore, attempts a new harmony by trying to show that the first chapter of Genesis gives only the order in which the creative words were uttered, not the order in which the resulting effects were produced. Unfortunately, in accomplishing this purpose, he, like his predecessors, reveals an almost complete disregard for the obvious meaning of the Genesis narrative.

After a close study of the Genesis narrative and the numerous attempts of harmonizing it with science, the present writer has become thoroughly convinced that it is impossible to establish a complete, detailed harmony between the Genesis account of creation and the established facts of science without doing violence to the Bible or to science or to both. The only harmony possible is what has been called an "ideal harmony," that is, a harmony not extending to details, but limited to salient features. But this gives away the very position for which the "harmonists" have contended. As Driver says, "If the relative priority of plants and animals, or the period at which the sun and moon were formed, are amongst the details on which harmony cannot be established, what other statement (in the account of creation) can claim acceptance on the ground that it forms part of the narrative of Genesis?"[21]

Admitting now the presence of discrepancies between science and the Old Testament, what becomes of the Old Testament?[22] Must it be dis-

carded as no longer "profitable for teaching, for
reproof, for correction, for instruction which is in
righteousness"? Some there are who seem to
fear such fate for the book they dearly love.
On the other hand, there are multitudes who
calmly admit the claims of science, and at the
same time continue to read and study the pages
of the Old Testament, assured that it can still
furnish nourishment to their spiritual natures.
This attitude of confidence has been made possible,
on the one hand, by a broader and truer conception of divine revelation, and, on the other, by
a more adequate interpretation of the purpose of
the Bible and of the biblical writers.

Believers in God have come to realize as never
before that God has spoken and still speaks in
a variety of ways. Manifestations of God may
be seen on every hand:

> The heavens declare the glory of God;
> And the firmament showeth his handiwork.
> Day unto day uttereth speech,
> And night unto night showeth knowledge.[23]

What is the universe but a manifestation of God?
The whole realm of nature is in a real sense a
record of divine revelations, which science seeks
to interpret. "Now," says A. H. McNeile,[24]
"If God created all things and carries the universe
along by the utterance of his power, it is clear
that every fresh item of knowledge gained by

scientific investigation is a fresh glimpse into the will of God. Strictly speaking, there is no such thing as secular knowledge. A man only makes his studies secular for himself as he divorces them from the thought of God, so that all the scientific experiments in the world form part of the study of one aspect of God's Word."

On the other hand the purpose of scripture has come to be more adequately apprehended. The New Testament makes it perfectly clear that the aim of the Old Testament Scriptures is to bring man into harmony with God, to make him morally and spiritually perfect, and to point to the consummation of the redemptive purpose of God in and through the Christ.([25]) There is no warrant anywhere for the belief that the Old Testament writers meant to teach science of any kind. This is admitted even by some who insist upon the accuracy of the scientific teaching of the Bible. "It is true that the Scriptures were not designed to teach philosophy, science, or ethnology, or human history as such, and therefore they are not to be studied primarily as sources of information on these subjects."([26]) Evidently, then, wherever the Old Testament touches upon questions of science it treats them only in so far as they serve a higher ethical or spiritual purpose. Is it necessary to have absolute scientific accuracy in every detail in order to do this effectively? A moment's thought will show that it is not. The writer heard not long ago a powerful appeal on behalf of the boys in a certain community, in which the speaker referred to the "Gracchi, the most renowned citizens of Athens." The historical inaccuracy in no wise affected the moral force of the appeal. No one would be foolish enough to assume that the spiritual and ethical value of sermons preached by the early Church fathers is invalidated by the fanciful science mixed with their gospel message. Who has not heard sermons that created a profound spiritual impression, though their science and history were not altogether faultless? It would seem, then, that in estimating extra-biblical utterances the principle is recognized that "ignorance of some departments of truth does not disqualify a man for knowing and imparting truth about God; that in order to be a medium of revelation a man does not need to be in advance of his age in secular learning; that intimate communion with God, a spirit trained to discern spiritual things, a perfect understanding of and zeal for God's purpose are qualities quite independent of a knowledge of the discoveries of science."[27]

Is it right to raise a different standard for the Scriptures? "Certainly," say many, "because the Bible is inspired; it is the Word of God, and God cannot inspire an untruth of any kind."

Now, it may be readily admitted that God cannot inspire an untruth; but have we any right to argue as if we knew exactly how God ought to convey a revelation to man? Without entering upon a discussion of the entire subject of inspiration, the question may be raised whether or not inspiration covers purely scientific information. The claim has been put forth by some who believe that the Bible and science are in perfect agreement that this agreement "proves that the scientific element of scripture as well as the doctrinal was within the scope of inspiration."[28] Consistency might seem to require the admission that disagreement would prove that the scientific element does not fall within the scope of inspiration. At any rate, it is of enormous importance to remember, what should be a perfectly obvious principle, that the facts presented in the Bible must determine the answer to the inquiry. In other words, "We can learn what the Bible is only from what the Bible itself says."[29]

One thing is quite certain, namely, that the Bible makes not the slightest claim of being a scientific treatise complete and up-to-date.[30] It is equally true that it does not deny being such a treatise, hence the inquirer is thrown back upon a study of the facts presented in the Bible; and upon the basis of these he must determine whether or not there is reason for believing that scientific knowledge comes within the scope of inspiration. Now, the abstract possibility of God communicating to man a knowledge of exact scientific facts in a prescientific age need not be denied. It is, however, a question whether God could have communicated such facts to man three thousand years ago without robbing him of his personality and changing him into a mechanism. So far as the ways of God are known from experience, observation, history, and other sources, he has always treated with respect and consideration the powers and faculties of his chief creature. "Had inspired men," says Dods,(31) "introduced into their writings information which anticipated the discoveries of science, their state of mind would be inconceivable, and revelation would be a source of confusion. God's methods are harmonious with one another, and as he has given men natural faculties to acquire scientific knowledge and historical information, he did not stultify this gift by imparting such knowledge in a miraculous and unintelligible manner." The same truth is expressed by H. E. Ryle in these words: "We do not expect instruction upon matters of physical inquiry from revelation in the written Word. God's other gifts to men, of learning, perseverance, calculation, and the like, have been and are a true source of revelation. But scripture supplies no short cut for the intellect. Where man's intellectual powers may hope to attain to the truth, be it in the region of historical, scientific, and critical study, we have no warrant to expect an anticipation of results through the interposition of supernatural instruction in the letter of scripture. . . . Scripture is divinely inspired, not to release men from the toil of mental inquiry, but to lead and instruct their souls in things of eternal salvation."[32]   This is not an arbitrary limitation of the scope of inspiration; it is a conclusion based upon a careful consideration of the facts of science and of the Bible, which seem to furnish sufficient evidence that the biblical writers were not in any marked degree in advance of their age in the knowledge of physical facts or laws.   In other words, the Bible is primarily a book of religion, hence religion, and not science, is to be looked for in its pages.   Altogether too much time has been spent in an effort to find in it scientific truth in a scientific form.   Such attempts clearly disregard the purpose of the biblical writers as interpreted in the New Testament.

And could a Divine Providence have chosen a different method?   Even now discoveries follow one another so fast in the realm of science that no book remains a standard work for more than a few years.   It seems obvious, therefore, that a book written thousands of years ago could not remain a standard scientific work for all times.

But assuming for the sake of argument that God had communicated the knowledge of scientific facts to these writers—evidence for which is entirely lacking—what would have been the result? Later occurrences suggest what might have happened. The great mass of people would have looked upon teachers of strange science as heretics and madmen, and would have rejected not only their scientific teaching but their religious teaching as well. What a loss that would have been to mankind! No serious loss would come to men if they were left a while longer in ignorance concerning scientific matters, but very serious loss would come to them by continuing in their lower religious and ethical beliefs and practices. The only way to make the higher religious truth understood was to present it in a form easily apprehended by the people. To do this is the chief purpose of the primitive, *prescientific science* of the Old Testament Scriptures.

The peculiar element in scripture is the spirit and religious atmosphere which permeate all its parts and give to the Bible a unique place among the literatures of the world. This is the divine element due to inspiration. It is this element which establishes a gulf between the Hebrew account of creation and the cosmologies of other nations. Though the biblical writers had very much the same idea about the form and general

arrangement of the visible world as we find among
other peoples—ideas that have satisfied at all
times the majority of men even among nations
with a pretense to culture, namely, the cosmology of appearances—these ideas were all
connected with their sublime faith in Jehovah:
to his omnipotence they referred the existence of
the world, and they made all its changes depend
entirely on his will.   In their monotheistic religion
they secured the foundation of a clear and simple
cosmology different from the grotesque cosmologies of other nations and yet not beyond
the demands of men of a primitive type and of
simple mind, who were full of a lively imagination,
but not much accustomed to analyze phenomena
or their causes.

In this connection it may prove helpful to
remember what, according to the biblical viewpoint and in the light of history, was the con-
tribution of Israel to the development of the
human race. "Israel," says G. W. Jordan,[33] "is
comparatively young, politically it is provincial,
socially it is not brilliant, in the realm of science
it is narrow and dependent; yet when we lay
stress on these limitations we only cause the
peculiar glory of this nation's life to stand out
more clearly; it has its own individuality; its
real leaders are men of genius, their ambition is
to speak in the name of the eternal king; they

hear the divine message and claim for it the supreme significance." This is the judgment of a Bible student. The same truth is expressed in the words of one who approaches the Bible from the viewpoint of the scientist, namely, the eminent Italian astronomer, Schiaparelli([34]): "Their [the Hebrews] natural gifts, as well as the course of events, carried them to a different mission [from that of Greece and Rome] of no smaller importance —that of purifying the religious sentiment and of preparing the way for monotheism. Of this way they mark the first clear traces. In the laborious accomplishment of this great task Israel lived, suffered, and completely exhausted itself. Israel's history, legislation, and literature were essentially coördinated toward this end; science and art were for Israel of secondary importance. No wonder, therefore, that the steps of the Jews' advance in the field of scientific conceptions and speculations were small and feeble; no wonder that in such respects they were easily vanquished by their neighbors on the Nile and the Euphrates."

In conclusion: Permanent harmony between science and the Bible will be secured when each is assigned to its legitimate sphere. Science has a right to ask that, if men are seeking purely scientific information, they should turn to recent text-books in geology, astronomy, or the other

sciences. But in the sphere to which Jesus and
the New Testament writers assigned the Old
Testament science cannot deny or seriously question its inspiration or permanent value. Un-
prejudiced science has never done this. It is
perfectly ready to recognize the inestimable religious and ethical value of even those Old Testament
narratives which refer to scientific facts, not
because of their scientific teaching, but because
of the presence of eternal truth in the crude form
of primitive science. Fair-minded scientists readily admit that if anyone wishes to know what
connection the world has with God, if he seeks
to trace back all that now is to the very fountain
head of life, if he desires to discover some unifying
principle, some illuminating purpose in the history
of the world, he may still turn to the early chapters of Genesis as a safe guide.

What, then, is the bearing of the conclusions
of modern science upon the permanent value of
the Old Testament? Science has compelled the
Bible student to withdraw the attention from the
nonessential and secondary, and to concentrate
it upon the heart and substance. In doing this
it has established upon a much firmer basis the
conviction that, whatever the scientific value of
scripture may be or may not be, the apostle was
right when he wrote that "the sacred writings . . .
are able to make wise unto salvation through

faith which is in Christ Jesus. Every scripture inspired of God is also profitable for teaching, for reproof, for correction, for instruction which is in righteousness: that the man of God may be complete, furnished completely unto every good work."([35])

NOTES ON CHAPTER II

([1]) Burgon, Inspiration and Interpretation, p. 89.

([2]) Presbyterian Review, 1881, p. 238.

([3]) Josh. 10. 12.

([4]) The Bible—Its Meaning and Supremacy, p. 160.

([5]) In a brief treatment it seems preferable to confine the discussion to a specific concrete case; therefore this chapter deals almost exclusively with questions centering around the subject of cosmogony.

([6]) The margin of the Authorized Version still gives the chronology of Archbishop Ussher to that effect.

([7]) Chapter IV, 1.

([8]) The Expositor, 1902, pp. 159, 160.

([9]) It requires but a reading of the "proofs" of the opposite view to understand their weakness. Compare Expositor, 1886, pp. 287–289.

([10]) The book of Genesis, p. 4.

([11]) Another difficulty has been found in the statement of Genesis that "vegetation" was complete two days before animal life appeared, but the disagreement is more apparent than real. The geological record, it is true, shows many more animal than plant remains in the very ancient rocks. It was not until Devonian and Carboniferous times that the plants became very abundant, as far as the geological records go. Indeed, in the oldest rocks in which animal remains occur, no plant remains have been discovered. However, this is not to be taken as proving that animals existed before plants, because low forms of the latter, having no hard parts, would be preserved with difficulty. Moreover, in some of the primitive forms, it is not easy to distinguish plants from animals. But, apart from the records in the rocks, both biologists and geologists believe that plants existed as early as animals, if not earlier, for the latter needed the former to live upon. An eminent geologist, Professor U. S. Grant, of Northwestern University, has expressed his opinion to the writer in these words: "It seems to me that, viewed in an abstract way, the Genesis statement of vegetation appearing before animal life is not far from correct."

[12] The Book of Genesis, p. 25.

[13] Natural Theology, Vol. I, pp. 229, 230.

[14] History of the Old Covenant, Vol. I, p. cxxix.

[15] The Testimony of the Rocks, Lecture IV.

[16] Reconciliation of Science and Religion, pp. 356ff.; compare also Pre-Adamites, *passim*.

[17] Origin of the World According to Revelation and Science, *passim*.

[18] Bibliotheca Sacra, 1885, pp. 201ff.

[19] The Conflict of Truth, pp. 162ff.

[20] Kurtz, Miller, Dawson, Dana, and the rest.

[21] Expositor, 1886, p. 38.

[22] The writer wants it clearly understood that an "ideal," harmony, as described above, can be established. He is equally certain, however, that the harmony cannot be carried into details.

[23] Psa. 19. 1, 2.

[24] Expository Times, October, 1907, p. 20.

[25] See above, Chapter I, p. 12.

[26] Presbyterian Review, 1881, p. 239.

[27] Marcus Dods, The Book of Genesis, pp. 4, 5.

[28] Presbyterian Review, 1881, p. 239.

[29] Expository Times, October, 1907, p. 20.

(30) Surely, there is not the slightest claim in Scripture that Moses or any other biblical writer received divine information concerning the beginnings of the universe; nor is there anything to support the assumption that the account of creation was supernaturally revealed to Adam, and that from him it was transmitted word for word through the families of the pious antediluvians, of Noah, Shem, Abraham, Isaac, Jacob, etc., until it was finally received and committed to writing by Moses.

(31) The Book of Genesis, p. 5.

(32) H. E. Ryle, The Early Narratives of Genesis, pp. 5, 6.

(33) Biblical Criticism and Modern Thought, p. 90.

(34) Astronomy in the Old Testament, p. 1.

(35) 2 Tim. 3. 15–17; on the permanent value and significance of the Genesis narratives; see also below, pp. 234ff.

CHAPTER III

The Old Testament and Modern Criticism

No careful observer can doubt that modern criticism has exerted a marked influence upon the attitude of many Christian people toward the Bible. Both those in sympathy with new ideas and those opposed to them frequently speak of the crisis which this criticism has brought about. "It does seem," says John E. McFadyen, a believer in the methods and results of modern criticism, "that the Church to-day in all her branches is face to face with a crisis of the most serious kind."[1]   On the other hand, John Smith, a determined opponent of criticism, writes concerning the conclusions of the latter: "They conflict with the profoundest certitudes of the faith, must inevitably alter the foundation on which from the beginning our holy religion has stood before the world, and, consequently, so far as a theory can, must obstruct her mission and abridge her influence."[2]   Whether the crisis is as acute as is here implied or not, there seems to be much concern among devout believers in the Bible about the bearing of modern criticism upon the value of the book they dearly love.   In the nature of the case, limitation of space forbids an exhaustive discussion of this interesting subject here. There are, however, three questions which are worthy of serious consideration: (1) What is modern criticism? (2) What are the more important conclusions of criticism that have secured wide recognition? (3) What is the bearing of these conclusions, if true, upon the Christian view of the Old Testament?

What, then, is biblical criticism? It is defined by Nash as "the free study of all the facts,"[3] which definition McFadyen expands so as to read, "the free and reverent study of all the biblical facts."[4] Criticism is *study*, which means careful investigation rather than superficial reading followed by hasty or unfounded conclusions. The investigation is *free* in the sense that though it is not disrespectful to traditional beliefs, it is not prevented by them from marking out new paths if the facts so demand. It is *reverent* because it deals with a book that has played a unique part in the religious life and thought of many centuries, and has been received as a book in which the voice of God may be heard. It is primarily a study of the *facts* presented by the book, not of theories or speculations, though in the study of these facts much may be learned from the theories of the past, and the study may give rise to new theories. In order to be thoroughly scientific, it must have due regard for *all* the facts in the case. For convenience sake it has become customary to distinguish four phases of Old Testament, or biblical, criticism: (1) Textual Criticism; (2) Linguistic Criticism; (3) Literary Criticism; and (4) Historical Criticism.

Close students of the Hebrew text of the Old Testament have been compelled to admit that even the oldest Hebrew manuscripts now known are not free from errors and blemishes, and it is the office of textual criticism to remove such errors by the use of all legitimate methods and means and to restore the *ipsissima verba* of the author. The presence of corruptions in the text is established by facts like these: (1) There are passages in which the text as it stands cannot be translated without violence to the laws of grammar, or, which are irreconcilable with the context or with other passages. For example, in 1 Sam. 13. 1 the Authorized Version reads, "Saul reigned one year, and when he had reigned two years over Israel." This translation does violence to the laws of Hebrew grammar. The Hebrew reads, literally, "The son of a year was Saul in his reigning," which may be rendered, "Saul was a year old when he began to reign." The narratives concerning events in the life of Saul before he became king make it clear that this statement is not correct. Perhaps the scribe, in writing the

formula, which is the usual formula for stating
a king's age at his accession, left a space for
the numeral to be filled in later, and forgot the
omission; or the numeral has accidentally dropped
out. In this case, it is the duty of textual criticism to supply, if possible, the age of Saul when
he was made king. In the absence of all external evidence the textual critic must fall back
upon conjecture. This the translators of the
Revised Version did, for in the English Revised
Version we find in brackets the word "thirty,"
in the American Revised Version "forty." In
this special case the assured results of textual
criticism are purely negative, in that they have
established the fact that the present text cannot
be correct. The attempt to restore the original text rests upon conjecture. (2) Parallel
passages differ in such a manner as to make it
certain that the variations are largely due to
textual corruption. A good illustration is seen
in Psa. 18, when compared with 2 Sam. 22. These
two passages were undoubtedly identical in the
beginning; but even the oldest existing manuscripts show more than seventy variants between
the two chapters. (3) Some of the ancient
versions contain readings which often bear a
strong stamp of probability and remove or lessen
the difficulties of the Hebrew text. For example,
in Josh. 9. 4, where the Hebrew reads, "And they

went and made as if they had been ambassadors,"
the Septuagint reads, "And they went and pro-
visioned themselves." The latter reading is sup-
ported by nearly all the ancient versions, and
seems more probable than that of the Hebrew
text. Another illustration of a similar character
is found in Psa. 22. 16c, which is translated by
both the Authorized and the Revised Version,
"They pierced my hands and my feet." This,
however, is not a translation of the Hebrew at
all, for it reads, "Like a lion, my hands and my
feet." In this case the New Testament, as well
as the Latin and Syriac translations, supports the
reading of the Septuagint. Passages like these,
in which the text has evidently suffered in the
course of transmission, might be multiplied a
hundredfold, and it is generally considered a
legitimate ambition to attempt the restoration of
the Hebrew text to its original form.

Linguistic criticism deals with difficult and
obscure passages. Sometimes the meaning of
single words or phrases is uncertain, as, for example,
in Isa. 53. 1, which reads, in the Authorized Version, "Who hath believed our report?" The
margin gives as alternatives for "report" the
words "doctrine" and "hearing." The Revised
Version reads, "Who hath believed our message?"
with a marginal note, "Or, *that which we have
heard*." In form the word translated "message"

is a passive participle, meaning, literally, "that which has been heard." Surely, no one would consider "report," "doctrine," "hearing," "message," etc., synonymous. It is the duty of linguistic criticism to determine the exact meaning of the word. Sometimes grammatical constructions are ambiguous. Very familiar are the words in Isa. 6. 3, "Holy, holy, holy, is Jehovah of hosts: the whole earth is full of his glory." The margin suggests as an alternative for the last clause, "the fullness of the whole earth is his glory," which might mean something entirely different from the ordinary rendering. There are other passages, some among the sublimest prophetic utterances, in which it is by no means clear whether the reference is to the past or to the present or to the future. There is, indeed, plenty of room for the most painstaking work of the linguistic critic.

The literary criticism concerns itself with the literary history of Old Testament books. The Bible may be more than a human production, but in outward form it has the appearance of an ordinary work of literature; and, so far as its history as a collection of literary productions is concerned, it has not escaped the fortunes or misfortunes of other ancient literary works. It is a well-known fact that extra-biblical books, religious and secular, have come down from the

distant past bearing the names of men who cannot
have been their authors; for example, the Gospel
of Peter, or the Ascension of Isaiah. Some
ancient books have been interpolated and added
to from time to time; for example, the Sibylline
Oracles, the religious books of the Hindus. Some
ancient books are compilations rather than original
productions; for example, the Diatessaron of
Tatian, or the religious books of the Babylonians,
which give abundant evidence of compilation.
The discoveries of these phenomena in extra-
biblical books naturally raised the question
whether similar phenomena might not be found
in the books of the Old Testament. It is the
duty of literary criticism to throw light on these
questions; to decide whether all the Old Testament
books are rightly ascribed to the men whose
names they bear, whether they are original productions or compilations from earlier material, and
whether any of the books have received additions
or interpolations in the course of their literary
history.

Hand in hand with literary criticism goes
historical criticism. The student of Old Testament
history seeks to trace the development of the
history of Israel by combining in a scientific
manner the historical material scattered throughout the Old Testament. In doing this he is
compelled to determine the value of the sources

from which he gathers information. To do this is the duty of historical criticism. It inquires, for example, whether the records are approximately contemporaneous with the events they record; if so, whether the writers were qualified to observe the events accurately, or to record and interpret them correctly; and, if the accounts were written a considerable time subsequent to the events recorded, whether they were colored in any way by the beliefs and practices of the time in which they were written or compiled. This line of investigation is almost thrust upon the Bible student by a comparison of the books of Kings with the books of Chronicles, which in many portions cover the same ground; and yet, there are marked differences between the descriptions of the two.

These are the different phases of criticism. Ordinarily, however, only two kinds are distinguished: the lower, or textual criticism, and the higher criticism. The aims of textual criticism are described above. The higher criticism combines the functions of literary and historical criticism, while linguistic criticism is considered a part of exegesis or interpretation, not a separate branch of Bible study. The legitimacy of textual criticism is universally recognized. Its importance in a comprehensive study of the Bible is clearly implied in these words of W. H. Green, a generation ago the best known defender of the traditional view of the Old Testament: "Its function is to determine, by a careful examination of all the evidence bearing upon the case, the condition of the sacred text, the measure of its correspondence with, or divergence from, the exact language of the inspired penman, and by means of all available helps to remove the errors which may have gained admission to it from whatever cause, and to restore the text to its pristine purity as it came from the hands of the original writers. . . . It is not an arbitrary but a judicial process, based on fixed and intelligible principles and conducted in a determinate manner, in which all the evidence is diligently collected, thoroughly sifted, and accurately weighed, and the decision given in accordance with the ascertained facts."(5)

No exception is taken to linguistic criticism as a legitimate part of exegesis, but at the mention of higher criticism many good men and women become greatly disturbed, for they seem to look upon it as a handmaid of Satan. A few expressions will illustrate the feeling with which some regard this kind of study: One writer says, "Neither hard times nor higher criticism nor infidelity . . . has any effect upon the sale of the Divine Scriptures." He evidently places higher criticism on a par with infidelity. Again: "The so-called higher critics, it is well known, are constantly trying to shake the faith of the Christian by telling him that the books of the Bible were not written by the men whose names are usually given as the human authors." Another writer declares that the higher critics allege that the Bible is "the off-spring of incompetence and fraud." One more quotation may suffice: "Higher criticism tends invariably . . . to absolute rationalism and the discrediting of inspiration." Now, if higher criticism is on a par with infidelity, if it declares the Bible to be the "offspring of incompetence and fraud," if it constantly tries to shake the faith of Christians, if it tends invariably to absolute rationalism and discredits inspiration—if it does these things, then the Christian Church may well look upon it with dread and alarm. Whether or not higher criticism is guilty of the things charged against it will probably appear in the further discussion, for from now on chief emphasis will be placed upon the bearing of the higher criticism on the Christian view of the Old Testament.

First of all, it may be well to define, if possible, the term "higher criticism." It is too often assumed by those who should know better, that the adjective "higher" exhibits the arrogance of those using it, who claim thereby an unwarranted precedence for their methods. This assumption is erroneous, for the adjective is used simply to distinguish this kind of criticism from the lower or textual criticism, which, since its purpose is to fix the exact text of a book, necessarily precedes the application of the processes of the higher criticism. The designation may be unfortunate, but thus far no clearer or less objectionable substitute has been found. But what is higher criticism? Higher criticism may be defined as a process of scientific investigation for the purpose of determining the origin, original form, and intended value of literary productions. It cannot be emphasized too strongly that higher criticism is nothing more than a process of study or investigation. It is not a set of conclusions respecting the books of the Bible; it is not a philosophical principle underlying the investigation; it is not a certain attitude of mind toward the Bible; it is not a theory of inspiration nor a denial of inspiration. Higher criticism is none of these things. It is simply a process of study to determine certain truths concerning literary productions.

Again, higher criticism, as a process of study, is not confined to the study of the Bible. It was applied to extra-biblical books long before there was any thought of applying it to the Old or New Testament. Eichhorn, who first applied the term to Old Testament study, has this to say: "I have been obliged to bestow the greatest amount of labor on a hitherto entirely unworked field: the investigation of the inner constitution of the separate books of the Old Testament by the aid of the higher criticism, *a new name to no humanist.*"(⁶)

Once more: the higher criticism as such is not opposed to traditional views. In the words of Professor Zenos: "Its relation to the old and the new views respectively is one of indifference. It may result in the confirmation of the old, or in the substitution of the new for the old. . . . It is no respecter of antiquity or novelty; its aim is to discover and verify the truth, to bring facts to light whether these validate or invalidate previously held opinions."(⁷) It is a grave mistake, therefore, to attribute to higher criticism an essentially destructive purpose. In reality, it has confirmed traditional views at least as often as it has shown them to be untenable. It does not approach its investigations even with a suspicion of the correctness of tradition; it starts out with the tradition, it accepts it as correct until the process of investigation has brought to light facts and indications which cannot be harmonized with tradition. In such a case criticism believes itself bound to supply a satisfactory explanation of the facts, though such explanation may be contrary to the claims of tradition. Any student who approaches the inquiry in a spirit differ-

ent from that here indicated introduces into
his investigation elements that are not a part of
higher criticism as such, and the latter cannot
and should not be held accountable for them.

That it is desirable to answer questions concerning the origin, form, and value of biblical
books no one will dispute. C. M. Mead, exceedingly cautious and conservative, says: "I regard
the higher criticism as not only legitimate but
as useful, and indiscriminate condemnation of it
as foolish. Genuine criticism is nothing but the
search after truth, and of this there cannot be
too much."([8]) No literary production in the
Bible or outside of the Bible can be fully understood unless the interpreter has a full knowledge
of its origin, its author, and its first readers.
When, where, by whom, to whom, under what
circumstances, for what purpose?—an answer to
these and similar questions will wonderfully illuminate the message of a book. A knowledge of
the form of the writing is also essential to a proper
understanding of the same. Is it history or
poetry? is it narrative or prediction? or any one
of the various kinds of literature? In a similar
manner it is important, though not always easy,
to know the value a given literary work was
intended to have. Is it to be understood as
literal history? Is its essential purpose didactic,
without special regard for historic accuracy in

every detail? Are the religious and ethical truths taught intended to be final, or do they mark a stage in the development toward perfection and finality? These and other important questions of a similar nature the higher criticism seeks to answer.

Some one may say, "Scholars in all ages have sought to answer these questions; why is it, then, that modern higher criticism reaches conclusions concerning the origin, form, and value of Old Testament writings not dreamed of a few centuries ago?" This is a legitimate question, but the answer is not far to seek. It may best be answered by asking another question: Men in all ages have studied the earth, the sun, the stars, and other phenomena of nature; how is it that modern scientists have reached conclusions unknown and undreamed of a few centuries ago? The modern higher criticism, like all modern science, is the outgrowth of the awakening during the Middle Ages which revolutionized the whole world of science, literature, and religion. The Renaissance aroused men's interest in literature and science, the Reformation aroused men's interest in religion as a personal experience. In the Renaissance men began to think for themselves in matters of science and literature; in the Reformation they began to think for themselves in matters of religion. It was inevitable that the awakening of thought and the substitution of reason for authority in science, secular literature, and secular history should ultimately affect sacred history and sacred literature as well.([9])

Chronologically, it is true, the work of higher criticism began even before the time of the Renaissance among Spanish Jews. But this Jewish criticism did not at the time exert any influence in the Christian Church. Only after criticism had secured a foothold among Christian scholars were the results of Jewish investigation made use of. In the same way the purely negative conclusions of some of the early Christian heretics, based upon dogmatic considerations rather than historical investigations, have no organic connection with the investigations and results of modern criticism. It is perfectly correct, therefore, to state that the modern higher criticism had its birth in the great awakening of the Renaissance and the Reformation. They gave to it a life and an impetus which from that day to this have not abated in the least. Some of the reformers themselves and their coworkers advanced views which later investigation has confirmed and expanded. Carlstadt, for example, the friend and coworker of Luther, published in 1520 an essay in which he argued, on the ground that the style of narration in the account of Moses's death which, he believed, was not written by Moses, was the same as in the preceding chapters, that it might be held that Moses did not write the entire Pentateuch. The freedom with which Luther criticized both the Old and the New Testament books is well known. Concerning the Old Testament, he admitted that the books of Kings were more credible than Chronicles. "What would it matter," he asks, "if Moses did not write the Pentateuch?" He thinks it probable that Isaiah, Jeremiah, Hosea, and Ecclesiastes received their final form at the hands of redactors. The testimony of the psalm titles he does not regard as conclusive. He admits chronological difficulties and contradictions in the statements of historical facts. He concedes that we do not always hear God himself speaking in the Old Testament. Esther might well have been left out of the canon, and First Maccabees might have been included. If this is not criticism, what is?

The case of Luther has been mentioned simply to show the absurdity of the claim that modern higher criticism is the outgrowth of German rationalism or English deism or infidelity; or that a man who pursues Old Testament study on the line of the higher criticism is necessarily an infidel, a rationalist, or a fool. True, there have been and are those out of sympathy with Christianity or the Bible who have employed critical methods in carrying on their anti-Christian warfare; but

such misuse of critical methods no more proves
the illegitimacy of this process of investigation
than the employment of a surgical instru-
ment, which, in the hands of a skillful surgeon,
may be the means of saving a diseased organism,
by a murderer to carry out his destructive aim,
would prove that the use of all surgical instruments is unscientific or criminal. The vast majority of the so-called higher critics do not deserve
the denunciations heaped upon them by some
who consider themselves sole defenders of the
faith. Most of them are Christian men whose
loyalty to Christ, whose devotion to the truth,
and whose sincerity of motive no one has reason
or right to question or doubt. It is exceedingly
unfortunate that many writers have failed to
recognize this fact. No one acquainted with the
history of biblical criticism can accept the following as a true characterization of serious critics: "I
mean by professional critic, one who spends his
time and strength in trying to find some error or discrepancy in the Bible; and, if he thinks he does, re-
joiceth as 'one who findeth great spoil'; who hopes,
while he works, that he may succeed, thinking
thereby to obtain a name and notoriety for himself."(¹⁰) In a similar spirit Sir Robert Anderson
speaks of "the foreign infidel type of scholar . . . as
ignorant of man and his needs as a monk, and as
ignorant of God and his ways as a monkey."(¹¹)

Such abuse is unchristian, and no good can be accomplished by it. The truth of the matter is more adequately expressed by James Orr when he says: "There are, one must own, few outstanding scholars at the present day on the Continent or in Britain—in America it is somewhat different—who do not in greater or less degree accept conclusions regarding the Old Testament of the kind ordinarily denominated critical. Yet among the foremost are many whom no one who understands their work would dream as classing as other than believing, and defenders of revealed religion."(12) Then, after mentioning a number of scholars, he describes them as "all more or less critics, but all convinced upholders of supernatural revelation."

But even among these Christian, evangelical, higher critics a distinction must be made between two classes. The one may be called, for want of a better name, traditional, because its adherents insist that their investigations on the line of the higher criticism have confirmed in all essentials the positions held during many centuries. It should be noted, however, that many scholars who are sometimes quoted as upholders of the traditional view are ready to make many concessions to those who believe that the traditional views are no longer tenable.(13) On the other hand is a class of critics which may be called nontraditional, critics who claim that their investigations, while confirming the truth of many traditional positions, compel them in other cases to set aside the traditional views in favor of some more in accord with the facts in the case. It may be difficult to state all the causes responsible for the differences in the conclusions of these two classes of critics. However, the writings of some scholars in the former class seem to show that the authors are influenced, to some extent at least, by the fear that further concessions would affect the Christian theory of inspiration. Another cause may be found in the fact that the present generation of Old Testament scholars received its training largely at the hands of those accustomed to the traditional viewpoint; the influence of this early training manifests itself to some extent in the present attitude. A more important cause, however, is supplied by the nature of the evidence upon the basis of which these critical questions must be settled. Mathematical demonstration is impossible in very many cases. The critic must be qualified to estimate probabilities, and various degrees of probability, depending upon the nature of the grounds on which it rests. In the nature of the case, the personal element enters into the estimate of the degree of probability. What to some may appear a high degree of probability, or amount to practical certainty, may to another investigator, perhaps less familiar with the facts in the case, appear of less value and lead him to reject the conclusion entirely. As long as this condition of affairs continues—and there is no reason to suppose that it ever will be otherwise—perfect agreement among critical investigators need not be expected; but a fair and thorough examination of the facts by all must be insisted upon.

It is not necessary to enlarge upon the views of the traditional class of critics, for theirs are the views with which most Christians now living have been familiar since their childhood. In order to understand, however, the bearing of the nontraditional criticism upon the Christian view of the Old Testament it is necessary to consider the most important conclusions of the nontraditional class of evangelical criticism; and to these conclusions we may now turn our attention.

1. Modern criticism has placed into clearer light the progressive character of Old Testament revelation. God is the same yesterday, to-day, and forever, but man has taken many advance steps; and as he advanced his spiritual capacities and powers of apprehension increased. This growth enabled him to secure, from generation to generation and from century to century, during the Old Testament dispensation, an ever-broadening and deepening conception of the nature and character of God and of his will. The Old Testa-

ment books, says Kent, are "the harmonious
and many-sided record of ten centuries of stren-
uous human endeavor to know and to do the will
of God, and of his full and gracious response to
that effort."[14]

2. Formerly the beginning of the Old Testament
canon was traced to Moses. He was thought not
only to have written the books of the Pentateuch
but to have given to them official sanction as
canonical books. To these books were gradually
added the other sacred writings of the Old Testament on the authority of the divinely chosen
successors of Moses, like Joshua, Samuel, and the
prophets. The close of the canon was ascribed
to Ezra, who, according to later views, had to
share the honor with the men of the Great Syna-
gogue. Modern criticism assigns new dates to
some of the Old Testament books; it believes
that the exile was a period of great spiritual and
intellectual activity, and a number of books are
placed subsequent to Ezra and Nehemiah, which
in itself would imply a denial of the view that
the canon was finally closed in the days of Ezra.
The modern critical view is that the Old Testament books were canonized—whatever the dates
of their writing—gradually and at a comparatively
late period. The canonization of the Law is
placed at about B. C. 400, that of the Prophets
between B. C. 250 and B. C. 180, while the third

division of the Jewish canon, the Writings, is believed to have acquired canonical authority during the second and first centuries B. C.

3. Formerly the order of the Old Testament books determined largely the view of the development of Hebrew religion. Just as in the New Testament the Gospels occupy first place, the Epistles being expositions of the principles laid down in the Gospels, so it was thought that the Law of the Pentateuch, coming from the hands of Moses, served as the basis of the religious development of the Hebrews during subsequent centuries. The prophets were looked upon chiefly as expounders and interpreters of this Law. Modern criticism has introduced a change of viewpoint. It does not deny the pre-exilic existence of all law, or of sacrifice, or of a ceremonial, or of other priestly elements, but it believes that in the religious development of Israel, the pre-exilic period was preëminently the period of the prophets, while the religious life during the post-exilic period was dominated by the priests, the priestly type of religion finding literary expression in the ceremonial system embodied in the Pentateuch.

4. According to modern criticism, compilation had a prominent place in the production of Old Testament books. The composite character of the Pentateuch is touched upon in the next paragraph, but, in addition, it is believed that

there is sufficient evidence to establish the composite character of practically all the other historical books. McFadyen accurately represents the modern viewpoint when he says, "In the light of all these facts the general possibility, if not the practical certainty, of the compositeness of the historical books may be conceded."([15]) Evidences of compilation are seen also in several of the prophetic books. The assignment of Isaiah and Zechariah to more than one author each furnishes perhaps the best known examples, but other prophetic books are similarly divided.

5. The Pentateuch is no longer assigned in its entirety to Moses; it is thought, rather, to contain material selected from four different sources, which the compiler had before him in writing.([16]) These documents did not reach their final form until some time subsequent to Moses, but all of them contained ancient material, much of it going back to the time of Moses, some of it even to pre-Mosaic days. Among the contents of the Pentateuch special attention is called to three legal codes—the Book of the Covenant, the Deuteronomic Code, and the Priestly Code—belonging to different periods in Hebrew history, and reflecting different stages in the religious and social development of the nation. The Deuteronomic Code, in some form, is believed to have been the basis of the reforms instituted by Josiah

and to have been written most probably during the early part of the seventh century. On these general questions respecting the Pentateuch there seems to be general agreement among critical scholars; on the other hand, there is wide divergence of opinion concerning points of detail, such as the chronological order in which the several documents reached their final form, their exact dates, the manner and time of their compilation, the detailed distribution of the material among the several sources, etc. The differences of opinion on these points are due to the fact that the data upon the basis of which the problems must be solved are not sufficiently numerous or decisive.

6. Doubt is thrown upon the authorship of a number of Old Testament books, or parts of books, which have been assigned to certain authors by both Jewish and Christian tradition. As already stated, the Mosaic authorship of the Pentateuch is denied; the book of Lamentation is taken away from Jeremiah; parts of Isaiah and Zechariah and the whole of Daniel are assigned to persons other than the prophets bearing these names. The accuracy of the psalm titles is questioned; few of the psalms, if any, are assigned to David or his age; and most of the psalms—by some scholars all—are placed in the post-exilic period. A conservative scholar, like W. T. Davison, is not willing to say more than " that

from ten to twenty psalms—including 3, 4, 7, 8, 15, 18, 23, 24, 32, and perhaps 101 and 110—*may* have come down to us from David's pen, but that the number can hardly be greater, and may be still less."([17]) The same uncertainty is believed to exist respecting the authorship of Proverbs and of Ecclesiastes, which is considered one of the latest books in the Old Testament canon. Other books, like Job, which in the absence of external testimony were formerly assigned to an early date, are now placed in the later period of Hebrew history.

In addition to these results touching upon matters practically unrecognized before, the higher criticism has emphasized some truths which, though known, exerted little, if any, influence upon the conception or study of the Old Testament. Of these perhaps the most important are, first, that the Old Testament is not so much a single book as a library consisting of many books of different dates and authorship, though all these books may be held together by one common spirit and purpose;([18]) and, second, that in these books are represented practically all the various forms and kinds of literary composition that can be found in the literatures of other nations.

These are perhaps the most important conclusions reached by the nontraditional higher critics. Some may not be willing to admit that these conclusions are well founded, and, indeed, the cautious among the critics very candidly state that in most cases scientific demonstration is impossible, that probability of varying degrees is an important element in the conclusions; but unless one has followed those who have reached the conclusions into every detail of their investigation, he is hardly competent to pass a valid judgment. And it is well to remember what seems to be an indisputable fact, that with very few exceptions Old Testament experts everywhere agree essentially on these results, and that an ever-increasing number of serious Old Testament students whose competency and sincerity cannot be doubted feel compelled to accept these conclusions, convinced that the traditional views cannot be maintained without numerous modifications. This fact may not establish the truth of these conclusions; nevertheless, it may serve as a sufficient reason for the consideration of another question: Should the truth of the conclusions enumerated be established beyond a possibility of doubt, what would be the effect upon the Christian conception of the Old Testament? What would become of its inspiration or authority, of the supernatural in its history, of the work and character of Moses, Isaiah, or David; and, perhaps most important of all, what effect would this have upon the authority of Jesus Christ himself?

The most important and vital of these questions may be considered first. How do the conclusions of the nontraditional higher criticism affect the authority of Jesus Christ? This question arises chiefly in connection with investigations into the authorship of Old Testament books, especially of the Pentateuch, the Psalms, and Isaiah. It is asserted that since Christ quotes and refers to passages from the books bearing the names of Moses, David, and Isaiah, apparently as if they had been written by these men, any claim that these passages were not written by the authors mentioned is an indication of unbelief, an insult to Christ, and a denial of his authority. "If Moses did not write the Pentateuch," says L. W. Munhall, "or any portion of it, and the highest critics (Jesus Christ and the Holy Spirit) declare he did, it would be a lie. It would be none the less a lie, even though the Jews held traditionally that Moses was the author of these books. The testimony of the *Highest Critics* is absolutely unerringly and eternally true, and he who hesitates to receive it as against all other testimonies is disloyal to the truth."[19] Clearly, this statement is based upon the assumption that Jesus gave deliberate decisions on questions of authorship, which assumption cannot be substantiated. In the first place, it is well to note that in less than one fifth of the New Testament quotations from the Old Testament is a personal name connected with the quotation; Jesus himself, in quoting from the Pentateuch and other Old Testament books, frequently omits all reference to the alleged author, which shows that he considered the question of authorship of no special significance in comparison with the truth taught. Moreover, in some cases at least, the exact form of quotation is doubtful. Compare, for example, Matt. 15. 4, "God said," with Mark 7. 10, "Moses said"; and Luke 20. 37, "Moses showed, in the place concerning the Bush," with Mark 12. 26, "Have ye not read in the book of Moses, in the place concerning the Bush how God spake unto him," with Matt. 22. 31, which, referring to the same statement, introduces it by, "Have ye not read that which was spoken unto you by God?" Which one of the evangelists has preserved the actual words of Jesus?

But even admitting that Jesus used in these and other passages a personal name, does this imply a decision respecting authorship? In extra-biblical literature no one would raise serious objection to the use of the name of a man to designate a book without implying that the man named was the author of the entire book. This is done also in the New Testament. In the sermon of Peter, "Samuel" evidently is used in the sense of "book of Samuel," for the reference is not to an utterance of Samuel but of Nathan,[20] and it cannot imply authorship, for some of the events recorded in First Samuel and those in Second Samuel occurred after Samuel's death. In the Epistle to the Hebrews,[21] a psalm is referred to as "David," which is not even by the title assigned to the great king of Israel.[22]   Might it not be, therefore, that "Moses" was used as a designation of a book, without a thought of authorship. This seems to be the case in 2 Cor. 3. 15: "Whensoever Moses is read, a veil lieth upon their heart."[23] All these facts suggest that while Jesus frequently quotes the Pentateuch, and in some cases connects the name of Moses with it, *he never does so to prove that Moses wrote it*.   W. T. Davison describes the situation correctly when he writes, "A study of the whole use of the Old Testament made by Christ in his teaching shows that the questions of date and authorship with which criticism is chiefly concerned were not before the mind of our Lord as he spoke, nor was it his object to pronounce upon them."[24]

But even admitting that the references of Jesus imply in some cases a recognition of authorship, the question still remains whether the few passages quoted carry with them the authorship of the entire book from which the quotations are made. There are even some conservative scholars who

answer this question in the negative. After
enumerating some of the passages referred to by
Jesus as coming from Moses, C. H. H. Wright
continues: "All, however, that can be fairly de-
duced from such statements is, the Pentateuch
contains portions written by Moses. It does not
follow that the five books as a whole were written
by that lawgiver."[25]   Though this explanation
seems satisfactory to some, others consider it
somewhat forced and unnatural, and they are
inclined to give different interpretations of the
words of Jesus.

Many hold that in his references to Old Testament books Jesus accommodated himself to the
usage of the Jews without indorsing their views
or giving expression to his own, even though he
knew that the commonly held opinions as to the
authorship of certain Old Testament books were
erroneous.   Those who advocate this view believe
that their attitude in no wise dishonors the Master.
Indeed, they say, one cannot easily see what
other course he could have taken. Jesus had
come to reveal the Father, to bring a fallen race
into harmony with a holy God. Surely, the task
was great, and there was but little time in which
to accomplish it. If he had turned aside from
his chief purpose to settle scientific and literary
questions which were not under discussion among
the people, he would have aroused popular opposi-

tion and thus have hindered his chief work. In no case do his references imply that he desired to pronounce an authoritative critical judgment, and in no case does the value of the quotation depend upon its authorship. Looking at the matter, therefore, from a pedagogical standpoint, it would seem that, in view of his important mission in the world, he was compelled to accommodate himself to the views of the people in all matters not essential to his work.

This view seems entirely satisfactory to many sincere Christian believers. There are, however, those who maintain that it would not have been legitimate for Jesus thus to accommodate himself to the usage of the people if he had known that their views were not in accord with the facts; nevertheless, they insist that his utterances do not settle purely literary questions. They believe that Jesus shared the views of the people, that he actually thought that Moses wrote the entire Pentateuch, and Isaiah, the whole of the book bearing his name; but that this was a limitation of knowledge on his part. And they further insist that this attitude toward Jesus in no wise affects the supreme and final authority of the Christ over the lives of men. The entire life of the Master, they say, shows that he regarded his mission as spiritual; he did not come to correct all errors, but merely those touching religion and ethics; and even here he did not give detailed specific rules. In many cases he simply laid down great principles, which in time might be worked out and applied to the details of human activity. He did not abolish slavery, he made no efforts to correct errors in science; why should he correct erroneous views respecting literary and critical questions? These were outside of his immediate sphere of interest. His knowledge or ignorance in these secondary matters does not necessarily involve his knowledge or authority in essentials.[26] Again, while Christ was God, he was also truly man. This union of the divine with the human, if real, must have brought some limitations. And the New Testament clearly teaches that in some respects the powers of Christ were limited. His omnipotence was limited, else he could not have felt hunger, weariness, pain, etc. As strength was needed, it was supplied. It may have been there potentially, but not actually. Might it not have been the same with omniscience? In one case, at least, Jesus admits that his knowledge was limited: "But of that day or hour knoweth no one, not even the angels in heaven, neither the Son, but the Father."[27] And, surely, that which, according to this admission, was hidden from Jesus was, as compared with a question of the authorship of a biblical book, of infinitely greater importance. It would seem, therefore, that B. P. Raymond is right when he says: "To affirm that he had knowledge of the critical questions which agitate Christian scholars to-day is to deny that he was made like unto his brethren. It is to compromise the reality of his humanity and to start on the road that leads to docetism. Fairbairn's conclusions are just; 'The humanity of the Saviour must be absolutely real.' "([28])

There are, then, three explanations of the references of Christ to the authorship of Old Testament books, each one of which seems perfectly fair, natural, and, above all, scriptural; and each one shows that his utterances do not finally settle purely literary questions. This conclusion, since it is in perfect accord with the New Testament, can in no wise be construed as an insult to the Christ, nor does it affect in the least the authority of Jesus in matters religious and ethical. What is said here of the words of Jesus is equally true, with some slight modifications, of similar New Testament references coming, not from Jesus directly, but from the authors of the New Testament books.

From the consideration of this question of vital interest we may turn to another, also of great importance, namely, what is the effect of critical conclusions upon the belief in the inspiration of the Old Testament, in the supernatural in its history, and in its authority? All these questions center in one, for inspiration implies the presence of a supernatural element, and the authority of the Old Testament depends upon the reality of its inspiration. Hence the real question is, Have the conclusions of the higher criticism disproved, or in any serious way affected, the reality of the inspiration of the Old Testament writers? This inquiry must be answered with an emphatic "No." Inspiration does not depend upon the fact that a certain definite individual is responsible for a writing. A book is inspired because God is back of it and in it, and not because a certain man wrote it. Nor does belief in inspiration depend upon the knowledge of the human author, else how could Christians believe in the inspiration of the men who wrote books like the Epistle to the Hebrews, the book of Job, the books of Samuel, and other biblical books whose authors are not named? Moreover, an inspired book does not lose its inspiration because it is discovered that the human agent inspired is one different from the man to whom tradition has been accustomed to assign the book. Would the laws of the Pentateuch be any less divine if it should be proved that they were the product of the experience of the chosen people from the time of Moses to the exile? Would the Psalms cease to lift us into the presence of God, if it should be demonstrated that most of them came from a period later than David? Is the book of Job less majestic and sublime because we know not the time or place of its birth? Are the Proverbs less instructive because criticism claims that they do not all come from the son of David?(²⁹)

Once more: inspiration is not confined to any form of literature; a parable may be as truly inspired as history; and the inspiration of a book does not vanish when it is assigned to one form of literature rather than to another. The conclusions of the legitimate higher criticism in no wise tend toward a denial of the inspiration of the Old Testament. Inspiration, the special divine providence over Israel, God's interference in the history of the chosen people, would stand out as prominently as ever if every claim of the higher criticism should be proved true. Most critical scholars are ready to indorse the words of Professor Sanday: "My experience is that criticism leads straight up to the supernatural, and not away from it."(³⁰) But if this be true, how can any authority which rightly belongs to the Old Testament be affected by criticism? This authority belongs to it by virtue of its inspiration, and the voice of God is not silenced by the conclusions of modern criticism.

"But," some one will say, "if this is true how is it that criticism has been and still is condemned unsparingly by many men whose sincerity and love for the truth cannot be called into question?" There are several reasons for this. In the first place even some very intelligent men seem to misunderstand both the purpose and the claims of the higher criticism. Another reason is that there are even among the evangelical critics those who lack judgment, and who permit themselves to draw inferences unwarranted by the facts in the case. As a consequence, ill-informed persons have concluded that all the results of criticism are unwarranted by the facts. A third reason is that some critics are arrogant and obnoxious in the presentation of their views, and, therefore, bring the entire process into disrepute. A fourth, and perhaps the most important, reason is that in addition to the legitimate higher criticism discussed in the preceding pages there is an illegitimate criticism which very frequently, though erroneously, is thought to be the only kind of criticism practiced. This criticism also studies the facts, but—and this is its distinguishing feature—its investigations are colored by certain presuppositions, such as the belief in a materialistic or deistic evolution, in the presence of which there is no room for inspiration, or for the supernatural, or for miracles, in the Christian sense of these terms. This kind of criticism is not legitimate, because it is not scientific, proceeding as it does on the basis of an unestablished, unchristian, and impossible view of the universe. But higher critics belonging to this class are few in number, and fairness and Christian courtesy demand that in any discussion of the subject clear distinctions should be made between this criticism and that process of investigation which is not only legitimate, but indispensable. It is also well to bear in mind that the conclusions of the illegitimate criticism will never be disproved by denunciation, but, rather, by the careful and painstaking labors of those critics who approach their studies without these unwarranted assumptions.

One more question remains to be considered, namely, What becomes of the men from whom criticism takes away at least part of the writings traditionally connected with their names? Preeminent among these are Moses, Isaiah, and David. Moses is not, as is sometimes erroneously asserted, removed to the realm of myths.([31]) To prove this assertion it is only necessary to quote the words of one who accepts the results of the higher criticism as set forth above: "Moses was the man who under divine direction 'hewed Israel from the rock.' Subsequent prophets and circumstances chiseled the rough bowlder into symmetrical form, but the glory of the creative act is rightly attributed to the first great Hebrew prophet. As a leader he not only created a nation but guided them through infinite vicis-

situdes to a land where they might have a settled
abode and develop into a stable power; in so doing
he left upon his race the imprint of his own mighty
personality. As a judge he set in motion forces
which ultimately led to the incorporation of the
principles of right in objective laws. As a priest
he first gave definite form to the worship of
Jehovah. As a prophet he gathered together all
that was best in the faith of his age and race,
and, fusing them, gave to his people a living
religion. Under his enlightened guidance Israel
became truly and forever the people of Jehovah.
Through him the Divine revealed himself to
Israel as their Deliverer, Leader, and Counselor—
not afar off, but present; a God powerful and
willing to succor his people, and, therefore, one
to be trusted and loved as well as feared. As
the acorn contains the sturdy oak in embryo,
so the revelation through Moses was the germ
which developed into the message of Israel to
humanity."([32])

Isaiah, though losing some of the sublimest
passages in the book, is still the king among the
prophets. In the words of Ewald, a pronounced
advocate of the conclusions of modern criticism:
"Of the other prophets all the more celebrated
ones were distinguished by some special excellence
and peculiar power, whether of speech or of
deed; in Isaiah all the powers and all the beauties

of prophetic speech and deed combine to form a symmetrical whole; he is distinguished less by any special excellence than by the symmetry and perfection of all his parts. There are rarely combined in one individual the profoundest prophetic emotion and purest feeling, the most unwearied, successful, and consistent activity amid all the confusions and changes of life; and, lastly, true poetic genius and beauty of style, combined with force and irresistible power; yet this triad of powers we find realized in Isaiah as in no other prophet."[33]

David, indeed, loses some of his halo, if many of the most beautiful psalms are taken from him, yet he remains the man after God's own heart. "According to his light, he served the Jehovah whom he knew with marvelous fidelity and constancy. . . . He ruled over the united Hebrew tribes as Jehovah's representative. In his name he fought the battles against Israel's foes, whom he regarded as Jehovah's also. . . . From the spoils which he won in his wars he provided the means wherewith to build a fitting dwelling place for the God of his nation. The priests found in him a generous patron, and prophets like Nathan were among his most trusted counselors. To do the will of Jehovah as it was revealed to him was the dominating principle of his life. More cannot be said of anyone."[34]

A splendid summary of the bearing of modern evangelical criticism upon the Christian view of the Old Testament is given by Canon Driver: "It is not the case that critical conclusions are in conflict either with the Christian creeds or with the articles of the Christian faith. Those conclusions affect not the *fact* of revelation but only its *form*. They help to determine the stages through which it passed, the different phases which it assumed, and the process by which the record of it was built up. They do not touch either the authority or the inspiration of the Scriptures of the Old Testament. They imply no change in respect to the divine attributes revealed in the Old Testament, no change in the lessons of human duty to be derived from it, no change as to the general position (apart from the interpretation of particular passages) that the Old Testament points forward prophetically to Christ. That both the religion of Israel itself and the record of its history embodied in the Old Testament are the work of men whose hearts have been touched and minds illuminated, in different degrees, by the Spirit of God is manifest."[35]

But not only has criticism not taken away anything essential from the Bible; on the contrary, it has resulted in some distinct gains. The textual criticism has furnished the modern student with a much more accurate text of the biblical books, while the linguistic criticism has established the interpretation of this text upon a firmer basis. The higher criticism also has made invaluable contributions toward a more adequate understanding of the Old Testament Scriptures. It has made impossible the arbitrary and, sometimes, unreasonable interpretations of scripture which in former ages have proved a serious detriment to religion and theology. It has restored to religious use some of the biblical books almost forgotten before, and endowed them with flesh and blood by throwing bright light upon the circumstances connected with their origin. It has made it possible to secure a "reasonable, probable, and even thrilling" view of the history and religion of Israel and of the steps by which the records of these grew up. Many of the moral, religious, and historical difficulties which served as effective weapons to skeptics in all ages have disappeared, and the weapons have been snatched from the enemies of the Bible. Many of the confusions and apparent discrepancies, which according to former theories presented insurmountable difficulties, have found a satisfactory explanation. "Higher criticism," says R. F. Horton, "so much dreaded by pious souls, is furnishing a conclusive answer to the untiring opponents of revelation."[36] Everyone knows that the Bible has been bitterly attacked in the past, and that such attacks have not altogether ceased even now; but it is sometimes overlooked that in the majority of cases these attacks are made by men who are, or seem to be, lamentably ignorant of the attitude and results of modern critical study. Their arguments become "absolutely powerless against the modern historical interpretation of the Bible; and the more that interpretation underlies the teaching of the young, the more certain are those attacks to die a natural death."([37])

There are, indeed, few Old Testament scholars who would not indorse the testimony of Professor A. S. Peake, given in a paper on "Permanent Results of Biblical Criticism," read before the Fourth Methodist Ecumenical Conference: "Speaking for myself, I may truthfully say that my sense of the value of Scripture, my interest in it, my attachment to it, have been almost indefinitely enhanced by the new attitude and new mode of study which criticism has brought to us."

NOTES ON CHAPTER III

([1]) Old Testament Criticism and the Christian Church, p. 1.
([2]) The Integrity of Scripture, p. 1.
([3]) The History of the Higher Criticism of the New Testament, p. 85.
([4]) Old Testament Criticism and the Christian Church, p. 47.

(⁵) General Introduction to the Old Testament: The Text, pp. 162, 163.

(⁶) J. G. Eichhorn, Einleitung in das Alte Testament, Preface to Second Edition.

(⁷) The Elements of the Higher Criticism, pp. 12, 13.

(⁸) Christ and Criticism, Preface.

(⁹) J. P. Peters, The Old Testament and the New Scholarship, p. 87.

(¹⁰) L. W. Munhall, Anti-Higher Criticism, p. 9. For a discriminating study of the theological and philosophical bias of the more representative Old Testament critics, see Bibliotheca Sacra, January, 1912, pp. 1ff.

(¹¹) The Bible and Modern Criticism, p. 19.

(¹²) The Problem of the Old Testament, pp. 7, 8.

(¹³) Some of these concessions are enumerated in J. E. McFadyen, Old Testament Criticism and the Christian Church, pp. 15ff. The Problem of the Old Testament, by James Orr, is often quoted as overthrowing entirely the positions of modern criticism regarding the authorship of the Pentateuch. If, however, one reads Orr's summary of the chief results of his own critical investigation (pp. 371ff.), the question may well be asked, Why should he be considered less of a higher critic than, for example, Wellhausen?

(¹⁴) The Origin and Permanent Value of the Old Testament, p. 30.

(¹⁵) Old Testament Criticism and the Christian Church, p. 143.

(¹⁶) Even those who question the existence of four independent documents assume the activity of at least four different hands.

(¹⁷) James Hastings, Dictionary of the Bible, Vol. IV, p. 151.

(¹⁸) See above, pp. 30ff.

(¹⁹) The Highest Critics vs. The Higher Critics, pp. 7, 8.

(20) Acts 3. 24. The passage in the mind of the apostle seems to be 2 Sam. 7. 11–16.

(21) Heb. 4. 7.

(22) Psa. 95.

(23) The origin of the designations Moses = Pentateuch, Samuel = books of Samuel, David = book of Psalms, must be explained, and can be explained; but as the mention of Samuel and David shows, it cannot always rest upon the fact of authorship, whatever the popular idea may have been.

(24) James Hastings, Dictionary of the Bible, Vol. IV, p. 151.

(25) Introduction to the Old Testament, p. 76.

(26) See above, p. 55.

(27) Mark 13. 32.

(28) M. S. Terry, Moses and the Prophets, p. 194.

(29) C. A. Briggs, General Introduction to the Study of Holy Scripture, p. 26.

(30) Quoted in J. E. McFadyen, Old Testament Criticism and the Christian Church, p. 253.

(31) Moses has, indeed, been removed by some investigators to the realm of myth, but not upon the basis of conclusions reached by the legitimate modern criticism.

(32) C. F. Kent, A History of the Hebrew People, Vol. I, pp. 44, 45.

(33) Prophets, English translation, Vol. II, p. 1.

(34) C. F. Kent, A History of the Hebrew People, Vol. I, p. 167.

(35) Introduction to the Literature of the Old Testament, pp. viii, ix.

(36) Revelation and the Bible, p. 61.

(37) J. E. McFadyen, Old Testament Criticism and the Christian Church, p. 136.

CHAPTER IV

THE OLD TESTAMENT AND ARCHÆOLOGY

A CENTURY ago the student of the world's history found it exceedingly difficult, if not impossible, to paint for himself a clear picture of events antedating B. C. 400. Concerning earlier periods, he was, aside from the Old Testament, practically without records that could claim contemporaneousness with the events recorded. But, one hundred years ago, men had commenced to test every statement, be it historical, or scientific, or theological, by severe canons of criticism, and if it could not stand the test, it was speedily rejected. One result of this tendency was to reject historical statements of the Bible when they could not be corroborated by reliable extra-biblical records. The nineteenth century has wrought a marvelous change. The Old Testament is no longer the "lone Old Testament," at the mercy of the scientific investigator. The historian and the Bible student now have at their command literary treasures almost without number, partly contemporaneous with the Old Testament, partly older by many centuries. These rich treasures have been brought to light by the perseverance and painstaking toil of archæologists, whose discoveries have shed light on human history during a period of more than four thousand years before the opening of the Christian era.

The historical movements recorded in the Old Testament, in which the Hebrews had a vital interest, were confined chiefly to the territory between the four seas of western Asia: the Mediterranean Sea, the Black Sea, the Caspian Sea, and the Persian Gulf. In the East the territory might be extended to include Persia; in the West, to include Asia Minor; and in the South or Southwest, to include Egypt, in North Africa. All these districts, which may be designated Bible lands, have been more or less thoroughly explored, and in most of them excavations have been carried on. The countries in which the most valuable finds, so far as Bible study is concerned, have been made are Palestine, Babylonia-Assyria, Egypt, Northern Syria, Phœnicia, Moab, and Asia Minor.

Even before excavations were undertaken travelers had visited these different countries and had reported their observations, but the information thus gained was more or less vague, and in many cases of no practical scientific value.([1]) They saw many strange mounds and ruins, and noticed and occasionally picked up fragments of inscriptions and monuments; but no one could decipher the inscriptions; hence the finds were preserved simply as mementoes and relics of an unknown age, from which nothing could be learned concerning the history and civilization of the people that once occupied these lands. The mounds and heaps of ruins which contained the real treasures were left undisturbed until the nineteenth century.

The pioneer in the work of excavation in the territory of Babylonia and Assyria was Claudius James Rich, who, while resident of the British East India Company in Bagdad, in 1811, visited and studied the ruins of Babylon, and a little later made similar investigations in the mounds marking the site of the ancient city of Nineveh. In the gullies cut by centuries of rain he gathered numerous little clay tablets, covered on every side with the same wedge-shaped characters as those seen on the fragments found by earlier travelers. These he saved carefully, and in time presented them to the British Museum.

No systematic excavations were carried on until 1842, when P. C. Botta was sent by the French government as vice-consul to Mosul on the upper Tigris. He noticed across the river from Mosul extensive artificial mounds which were supposed to mark the site of the city of Nineveh. These so aroused his curiosity that he began digging in the two most prominent mounds. Failing to make any discoveries, he transferred, the following year, at the suggestion of a peasant, his activities to Korsabad, a few miles to the northeast, where the digging produced, almost immediately, startling results. In the course of his excavations he laid bare a complex of buildings which proved to be the palace of Sargon, king of Assyria from B. C. 722 to B. C. 705, a palace covering an area of about twenty-five acres. The walls of the various buildings were all wainscotted with alabaster slabs, upon which were representations of battles, sieges, triumphal processions, and similar events in the life of ancient Assyria. He also found, in the course of the excavations, scores of strange figures and colossi, and numerous other remains of a long lost civilization. Botta's discoveries filled the whole archæological world with enthusiasm.

Even before Botta reached Mosul, a young Englishman, Austin Henry Layard, visited the territory of ancient Assyria, and was so impressed by its mounds and ruins that he resolved to examine them thoroughly whenever it might be in his power to do so. This resolution was taken in April, 1840, but more than five years elapsed before he began operations. It would be interesting to follow Layard's work as described by him in a most fascinating manner in Nineveh and Its Remains, and other writings, which give complete records of the wonderful successes he achieved wherever he went.

Never again did the labors entirely cease, though there were periods of decline. Layard's operations were continued under the direction of Rassam, Taylor, Loftus, and Henry C. Rawlinson; the French operations were in charge of such men as Place, Thomas, Fresnell, and Oppert. However, it was not until 1873 that other startling discoveries were made, chiefly under the direction of George Smith, who was sent by the Daily Telegraph, of London, to visit the site of Nineveh for the purpose of finding, if possible, fragments of the Babylonian account of the Deluge, parts of which he had previously discovered on tablets that had been shipped to the British Museum. In 1877 France sent Ernest de Sarzec as consul to Bosra in Lower Babylonia. His interest in archæology led him to investigate some of the mounds in the neighborhood, and he soon began work at one called Telloh. In the course of several campaigns, which continued until 1894, he unearthed a great variety of material illustrative of primitive ages, among his treasures being palaces, statues, vases, thousands of tablets, and various other articles of interest.

The first steps toward sending out an American expedition for excavation were taken at a meeting of the American Oriental Society in the spring of

1884. In the fall of the same year a preliminary expedition of exploration was sent out, which completed its labors during the winter and spring, returning in June, 1885. But the means for excavation were not forthcoming until 1888, when a well-equipped expedition was sent out under the auspices of the University of Pennsylvania. Four successive campaigns were carried on upon the great mounds of Nuffar, the site of Nippur, a center of early Babylonian life. Each expedition brought to light architectural and artistic remains and many thousands of tablets, throwing light upon all sides of the ancient life and civilization, over which hitherto there had lain almost complete darkness. In 1899 Germany sent its first expedition to Babylon and, during successive seasons, extensive excavations have been carried on, which have resulted in the discovery of many interesting finds. At a later date excavations were begun and, like those of Babylon, are still continued, on the mound covering the site of the ancient capital city of Assyria, Asshur, where inscriptions of great value have been uncovered. At the present time the Germans are perhaps the most active excavators in Assyria-Babylonia, and by their painstaking care to record every new discovery they are bound to increase the knowledge of the early history and civilization of these ancient empires.(²)

Reference may be made also to the later excavations of the French at Susa, the scene of the book of Esther, where they have uncovered much valuable material. The most important find, made in the winter of 1901–1902, is the monument upon which is inscribed the legal code of Hammurabi, king of Babylon, generally identified with the Amraphel of Gen. 14. 1. For a short time the University of Chicago carried on excavations at Bismiyah, in southern Babylonia, which have brought to light many objects of interest, if not of great historical importance. The Turkish government, under whose rule the territory of Babylonia and Assyria now is, stimulated by the example of other nations, is taking an active interest in these excavations, granting the privilege of excavating to an ever-increasing number of scholars, and giving them protection while engaged in their work. The Sultan has erected in Constantinople a magnificent museum, where the valuable antiquities are accessible to the scholarship of the world.

The credit of having first turned the attention of the West toward the monuments of Egypt, and of having brought them within the reach of science, belongs to the military expedition of Napoleon Bonaparte, undertaken in the summer of 1798.([3]) In August, 1799, a French artillery officer, Boussard, unearthed at the Fort Saint Julien, near

Rosetta, in the Nile Delta, a stone of black granite, three feet five inches in height, two feet four and one half inches in width, and eleven inches in thickness. It is thought to have been at least twelve inches higher and to have had a rounded top. On the upper portion of this block could be seen parts of fourteen lines of characters, resembling those seen everywhere on the obelisks and ruined temples of the land; adjoining these below are thirty-two lines of another species of script, while at the bottom are fifty-four lines, twenty-eight of them complete, in Greek uncial letters. The Greek was easily read, and told the story of the stone: It was set up in B. C. 195, by the priests of Egypt, in honor of Ptolemy Epiphanes, because he had canceled arrearages of certain taxes due from the sacerdotal body. The grateful priests ordered the memorial decree to be inscribed in the sacred characters of Egypt, in the vernacular, and in Greek. The Greek portion having been read, it was conjectured that the two inscriptions above the Greek told the same story. Such being the case, the value of the document for the decipherment of the Egyptian inscriptions was at once perceived, and scholars immediately set to work on the task of deciphering the unknown script. The honor of having solved the mystery belongs to François Champollion, who by 1822 had succeeded in fixing the value of a considerable portion of the ancient Egyptian signs, and at the time of his death, ten years later, left behind in manuscript a complete Egyptian grammar and vocabulary.

Through the discovery of Champollion the interest in ancient Egypt grew in all learned circles, and from his day until now efforts at bringing to light the remains of the Egyptian civilization have never ceased. The French have been especially active; but other nations also have been in the field and have greatly added to our knowledge of ancient Egypt. Since 1883 the Egyptian Exploration Fund has been at work in various parts of the Nile valley; private subscriptions have enabled the investigation of certain places of special interest; and now every year new finds are made, which constantly enrich our knowledge of the history, art, and civilization of the land of the Pharaohs.

"Palestine," says Dr. Benzinger, "became the object of most general interest earlier than any other Oriental country. . . . Nevertheless, Palestine research is but a child of the century just closed, the systematic exploration of the land, in all its aspects, beginning properly speaking with the foundation of the English Palestine Exploration Fund in 1865."([4] The reason for this delay is not far to seek. From the time that Christians first began to visit Palestine to a comparatively recent date all pilgrimages were prompted by religious, not by scientific motives. The interest of the pilgrims was excited only by those places which were pointed out to them as the scenes of sacred events, and the knowledge they brought home consisted chiefly of descriptions of the places held in special veneration. In 1841 there appeared in three volumes a work entitled Biblical Researches, in which Professor Edward Robinson recorded the results of his travels in Palestine during the year 1838. In 1852 Robinson made a second journey. During these two trips he and his companions worked with ceaseless industry, always accurately measuring the distances, and describing the route, even to the smallest detail. This painstaking care made the accounts so valuable that his books marked a turning point in the whole matter of Palestinian research, and could serve as a foundation upon which all future researches might rest.

Among other travelers who have made valuable contributions to our knowledge of Palestine, the most important are Titus Tobler, H. V. Guérin, E. Renan, and G. A. Smith. But the better the land came to be known, the more fully was it realized that the complete systematic exploration of the land was beyond the power of individual travelers. Hence in 1865 a number of men interested in Palestinian research met in London and organized a society known as the Palestine Exploration Fund. Its object was the complete, systematic, and scientific exploration of the Holy Land, especially for the purpose of elucidating the Scriptures. The idea was taken up with great enthusiasm, and from the beginning until now the society has been actively engaged in illuminating Palestine past and present. During the early history of the Fund few excavations were carried on, and these were confined to the city of Jerusalem; but since 1890 several mounds in southern Palestine have been excavated, the most important being Tel-el-Hesy, the probable site of ancient Lachish, and the site of the important city of Gezer. At present (1912) the site of ancient Beth-Shemesh is being excavated.

The German Palestine Society was organized in 1877 for a similar purpose. When the English surveyors were prevented by the Turkish government from completing the survey of eastern Palestine the German society took up the work, and its results are embodied in a map now in process of publication. The principal excavations of the German society were carried on between 1903 and 1907 at Tel-el Mutasellim, the ancient Megiddo, under the direction of Dr. Benzinger and Dr. Schumacher. Dr. Sellin carried on excavations at the neighboring Taanach for the Austrian government between 1902 and 1904.

Two other sites have been excavated—Jericho by the Germans and Samaria by Harvard University, and though no epoch-making finds have come to light in these two places, the results illuminate the early history of Palestine.

Phœnicia has yielded some of its treasures. The first of importance, found in 1855 in the Necropolis of Sidon, was the sarcophagus of Eshmunazar, king of Sidon. Since then various other sites have been examined, and much material has been unearthed, throwing light on the history, religion, art, and civilization of these ancient neighbors of Israel. In the year 1868 a German missionary, the Rev. F. Klein, discovered at Diban, the site of an ancient royal city of Moab, a large stone, with an inscription of Mesha, a king of Moab in the ninth century B. C. Between 1888 and 1891 investigations were conducted, for the Royal Museum in Berlin, at the mound of Zenjirli, once a city in the land Shamal, near the northern limits of Syria, south of the Issus, about forty miles inland. The old citadel was uncovered, and various sculptures, showing Hittite influence, a magnificent statue of Esarhaddon, king of Assyria, a huge statue of the god Hadad, and several Aramaic inscriptions of great value, as illustrating early Syrian civilization, were found. More recently, in 1906 and 1907, Professor Winckler visited Boghaz-koei, in Asia Minor, a center of early Hittite civilization, where he uncovered thousands of tablets which throw new light upon the history of western Asia in ancient times. Thus, generation after generation, amid dangers and hardships, a body of enthusiastic, self-sacrificing men have toiled almost day and night in order to restore to life a civilization buried for many centuries beneath the sands of the desert and the ruins of ancient cities, and we are only at the beginning. What revelations the next fifty years may have in store!

The results of these expeditions have been enthusiastically welcomed by all who are interested in antiquity: the students of history, art, science, anthropology, early civilization, and many others. They are, however, of special interest to the Bible student; and it is well to remember that, whatever additional motives may be responsible for excavations at the present time, from the beginning until now the desire to find illustrations, or confirmations of scriptural statements, has played a prominent part. "To what end," says Professor Delitzsch,([5]) "this toil and trouble in distant, inhospitable and danger-ridden lands? Why all this expense in ransacking to their utmost depths the rubbish heaps of forgotten centuries, where we know neither treasures of gold nor of silver exist? Why this zealous emulation on the part of the nations to secure the greatest possible number of mounds for excavation? And whence, too, that constantly increasing interest, that burning enthusiasm, born of generous sacrifice, now being bestowed on both sides of the Atlantic upon the excavations in Babylonia and Assyria? One answer echoes to all these questions, one answer which, if not absolutely adequate, is yet largely the reason and consummation of it all— the *Bible*."

Our purpose is to discuss the bearing of recent researches in Bible lands upon the Christian view of the Old Testament, that is, the view which looks upon the Old Testament as containing records of divine revelations granted in divers portions and in divers manners to the people of Israel. Concerning this bearing, two distinct and opposing claims are made: on the one hand, it is said that archæological research only confirms the familiar view of the Bible as a trustworthy and unique record of religion and history; on the other hand, it is claimed that archæological research has shown the Old Testament to be untrustworthy as to history, and as to religion, what has hitherto been regarded as original with the Hebrews is claimed to have been borrowed almost bodily from the surrounding nations.

What is the true situation? The archæological material which has more or less direct bearing upon our inquiry may be roughly arranged under two heads: (1) The Historico-Geographical; (2) The Religio-Ethical. The present chapter deals with the bearing of the historico-geographical material upon the Old Testament historical records, the other class being reserved for the succeeding chapter. The next step in the discussion will be to enumerate at least the more important finds having a more or less direct relation to the Old Testament. Many archæological objects have been brought to light, which, though they have but indirect bearing upon the Old Testament, have wonderfully illuminated the life of the ancient East, and thus have made more distinct the general historical background upon which the scenes recorded in the Old Testament were enacted. But a more important source of information are the inscriptions which have been discovered by the thousands and tens of thousands. These inscriptions were written on all kinds of material —granite, alabaster, wood, clay, papyrus, etc.; shaped in a variety of forms—tablets, cylinders, rolls, statues, walls, etc.; and they have been dug out of mounds, tombs, pyramids, and many other places. What, then, are the most important finds?

The first thing to bear in mind is that the inscriptions have very little to say about the earlier period of Hebrew history. Says Driver,([6]) "With the exception of the statement on the stele of Merneptah, that 'Israel is desolated,' the first

event connected with Israel and its ancestors
which the inscriptions mention or attest, is
Shishak's invasion of Judah in the reign of Reho-
boam; and the first Israelites whom they specify
by name are Omri and his son Ahab." Before
considering the statement on the stele of Merneptah, attention may be given to certain inscriptions
which throw considerable light on conditions in
Palestine before the Hebrew conquest, namely,
the so-called Tel-el-Amarna tablets.([7]) These tablets were discovered by accident in the winter
of 1887–1888 at Tel-el-Amarna, the site of the
ancient capital of Amenophis IV of Egypt, about
midway between Memphis and Thebes. On examination they proved to be a part of the official
archives of Amenophis III (1411–1375) and
Amenophis IV (1375–1358), consisting almost
entirely of letters and reports addressed to these
two Pharaohs by their officials in western Asia,
and by rulers who sustained close relations to
the Egyptian court. The royal letters, about
forty in number, are chiefly from kings of the
Hittites, of the Mitanni, of Assyria, and of Babylonia. The rest of the correspondence, about two
hundred and fifty letters, is of much greater
historical interest; it consists of letters from
Egyptian governors in various cities of Palestine,
Phœnicia, and Syria.

These inscriptions show that about B. C. 1400,

about two hundred years before the Hebrew conquest, Palestine and the neighboring countries
formed an Egyptian province under the rule of
Egyptian governors stationed in all principal
towns. At the time the Egyptians had considerable difficulty in maintaining their authority.
Their power was threatened by the Hittites and
other powerful neighbors, by the dissatisfied
native population, by the Habiri, who seem to have
been invaders from the desert, and by the intrigues
and rivalries of the Egyptian governors themselves.
Practically all the principal cities of the land are
mentioned in these letters. From the standpoint
of Old Testament study, six letters written by
Abdi-hiba, Governor of Jerusalem, are of special
interest. He, like many of the other governors,
is in difficulty. The Habiri are pressing him hard;
the neighboring cities of Gezer, Lachish, and
Askelon are aiding the enemy; he has been slan-
dered before the king and accused of disloyalty.
In the letters he emphatically protests his innocence. One of them reads: "To the king my lord,
say also thus: It is Abdi-hiba, thy servant; at
the feet of my lord the king twice seven times,
and twice seven times I fall. What have I done
against the king my lord? They backbite, they
slander me before the king my lord, saying:
Abdi-hiba has fallen away from the king his lord.
Behold, as for me, neither my father nor my

mother set me in this place; the arm of the mighty
king caused me to enter into the house of my
father. Why should I commit a sin against the
king my lord?"

Perhaps the most surprising fact about these
letters is that the Palestinian governors used, in
the correspondence with their superiors in Egypt,
not the Egyptian or native Canaanite, but the
Babylonian language, which seems conclusive
evidence that for some time previously Western
Asia had been under Babylonian influence. Without doubt this influence was primarily political,
but naturally it would bring with it elements of
civilization, art, science, and religion. Now and
then words in the Canaanite language occur,
either independently, or for the purpose of explain-
ing a Babylonian expression in the more familiar
dialect of the scribe. These Canaanite words are
hardly distinguishable from the Hebrew of the
Old Testament. It is evident, therefore, that the
pre-Israelite inhabitants of Palestine were closely
akin to the Hebrews, and spoke substantially the
same language. The inscriptions of later Egyptian
kings, during the thirteenth and the early part
of the twelfth century, throw little additional
light on conditions in Palestine, except that it
becomes increasingly clear that Egypt cannot
maintain its hold on the land. Subsequent to
Rameses III (1198–1167) Palestine was entirely

lost to Egypt for several centuries, which explains why the Hebrews were not disturbed by the empire on the Nile in their attempts to establish themselves in Palestine.

The first direct reference to Israel in the inscriptions apparently takes us near the time of the exodus. Archæology has nothing to say directly about the exodus; but in the enumeration of his victories, Merneptah II, thought to be the Pharaoh during whose reign the exodus took place, uses these words: "Israel is lost, his seed is not." The discovery of this inscription in 1896 was hailed with great rejoicing, for at last the name "Israel" was found in an Egyptian inscription coming, approximately at least, from the time of the exodus; but, unfortunately, the reference is so indefinite that its exact significance and bearing upon the date of the exodus is still under discussion. It is to be noted that, whereas the other places or peoples named in the inscription have the determinative for "country," "Israel" has the determinative for "men"; perhaps an evidence that the reference is not to the land of Israel, or to Israel permanently settled, but to a tribe or people at the time without a settled abode. But where was Israel at the time? To this a variety of answers have been given. D. R. Fotheringham suggests that the reference is to the destruction of the crops of Israel in Goshen.

Israel, he thinks, had just left, with the crops
unharvested. These Merneptah claims to have
destroyed.([8]) Others believe that the Israelites
had already entered Canaan when they suffered
the defeat mentioned by Merneptah. Petrie
thinks that the Israelites defeated were in Palestine,
but that they had no connection with the tribes
that had a part in the biblical exodus; he believes
that the latter were still in Goshen at the time
of this defeat.([9]) Still others believe that the
Israelites were, at the time of the defeat, in the
wilderness south of Palestine, and that the claim
of Merneptah is simply an attempt to account for
their disappearance from Egypt. And now comes
Eerdmans, of Leiden, with the suggestion that
the Israelites defeated by Merneptah were the
Israelites before they went down to Egypt.([10]) It
is seen, therefore, that the reference on the stele
of Merneptah, while of much interest, because it
is the first mention of Israel in an Egyptian inscription, after all throws little light upon the date
and the events of the exodus.

The next monument of importance contains an
account of the invasion of Palestine by Shishak, five
years after the death of Solomon. On the southern
wall of the court of the great temple of Amen at
Karnak the king has left a pictorial representation
of his campaign. A giant figure is represented as
holding in his left hand the ends of ropes which

bind long rows of captives neck to neck. Their
hands are tied behind them, and the victor's right
hand holds a rod with which he threatens them.
The names of the conquered cities are inscribed
on shields that cover the lower part of the body
of each prisoner. Some of the most familiar
names in this list are Gaza, Abel, Adullam, Beth-
horon, Aijalon, Gibeon, and Shunem.[11]

From about the middle of the ninth century
on inscriptions containing references to kings of
Israel, or to events in which the Hebrews played
important parts, become more numerous. To the
reign of Omri (889–875) and his immediate successors refers the inscription of Mesha on the so-
called Moabite Stone.[12] This notable specimen
of antiquity is a stone of a bluish-black color,
about two feet wide, nearly four feet high, and
fourteen and one-half inches thick; rounded at the
top, and, according to the testimony of the dis-
coverer, the Rev. F. Klein, also at the bottom,
which, however, is doubtful. The value of the
stone lies not only in the fact that it preserves
one of the most ancient styles of Hebrew writing,
but more especially in the historical, topographical,
and religious information it furnishes. In 2 Kings
3 we read of the relations between Moab and
Omri and his successors. Omri had subdued Moab
and had collected from her a yearly tribute. Ahab
had enjoyed the same revenue, amounting during

Mesha's reign to the wool of a hundred thousand lambs and a hundred thousand rams. At the close of Ahab's reign Mesha refused to continue the payment of the tribute. The allied kings of Israel, Judah, and Edom marched with their armies against the Moabites, who fled for refuge within the strong fortress of Kir-hareseth, where Mesha offered up his own son as a burnt-offering to Chemosh, his god; whereupon "there was great wrath against Israel, and they departed from them and returned to their own land."

The Moabite Stone was set up by King Mesha to his god Chemosh in commemoration of this deliverance. The opening lines read: "I am Mesha, son of Chemosh-ken, king of Moab, the Daibonite. My father reigned over Moab for thirty years, and I reigned after my father. And I made this high place for Chemosh in Korḥah, a high place of salvation, because he had saved me from all the assailants, and because he had let me see my desire upon all them that hated me. Omri, king of Israel, afflicted Moab for many days, because Chemosh was angry with his land; and his son succeeded him; and he also said, I will afflict Moab. In my days said he thus. But I saw my desire upon him and his house, and Israel perished with an everlasting destruction." As a supplement to the Old Testament narrative, his account is very instructive. The mention of

Yahweh, the God of Israel, is of interest, as also the fact that in Moab, as in Israel, national disaster was attributed to the anger of the national deity. The idiom in which the inscription is written differs only dialectically from the Hebrew of the Old Testament. Small idiomatic differences are observable, but, on the other hand, it shares with it several distinctive features, so that, on the whole, it resembles Hebrew far more closely than any other Semitic language now known. In point of style the inscription reads almost like a page from one of the earlier historical books of the Old Testament.

From the time of Omri on Israel came into frequent contact with Assyria; indeed, the fortunes of Israel were closely bound up with the fortunes of this great Eastern world-power.[13] In 885, at about the time when Omri had finally succeeded in overcoming his rivals, Ashurnasirpal ascended the throne of Assyria. He determined to restore the former glory of his nation, which had become eclipsed under his incompetent predecessors; and with him began a period of conquest which ultimately brought the whole eastern shore of the Mediterranean under Assyrian sway. In 860 Shalmaneser III[14] succeeded his father upon the throne of Assyria, and in the following year he renewed the attack upon the West. In 854 he felt prepared for a supreme effort, and it is in the

account of this campaign that we read for the
first time the name of an Israelite king in the
Assyrian inscription. Shalmaneser advanced with
great speed and success until he reached Karkar,
near the Orontes, a little north of Hamath. In
the account of the campaign he mentions, among
the allies who fought against him, Ahab of Israel,
who, he says, furnished two thousand chariots and
ten thousand men. The campaign is recorded in
several inscriptions, in all of which Shalmaneser
claims a complete victory.

The most famous inscription of this king is the
one on the so-called Black Obelisk, an alabaster
monolith found at Nimrud in 1846. This monument is inscribed on all four sides with an account,
in one hundred and ninety lines, of the expeditions undertaken during thirty-one years of the
king's reign. In the text of the inscription
reference is made to campaigns against the west
land (Syria and Palestine) in 859, 854, 850, 849,
846, 842, and 839. In addition to the inscription
the monument contains, on the upper portion,
five series of four reliefs each, each series representing the tribute brought to the Assyrian king by
kings whom he had conquered or who sought his
favor. In the inscription itself, no mention is
made of Israel or the king of Israel, but the second
tier of reliefs is of much interest. It depicts a
prince or deputy prostrating himself before Shal-

maneser, and behind the prostrated figure are attendants bearing gifts of various kinds. The superscription reads: "The tribute of Jehu, son of Omri, silver, gold, a golden bowl, a golden ladle, golden goblets, golden pitchers, lead, a staff for the hand of the king, shafts of spears, I received of him." In 842 Shalmaneser undertook an expedition against Hazael of Damascus, and in the account of this expedition he says, "At that time I received the tribute of the Tyrians and Sidonians, and of Jehu, the son of Omri."

About half a century after the occurrence of Jehu's name in the inscription of Shalmaneser III Israel is mentioned again as tributary to Assyria. Adad-nirari IV (812–783), after enumerating other countries subjugated by him, writes: "From the Euphrates to the land of the Hatti, the west country in its entire compass, Tyre, Sidon, the land of Omri, Edom, Philistia, as far as the great sea of the setting of the sun (Mediterranean Sea), I subjected to my yoke; payment of tribute I imposed upon them."

Adad-nirari was succeeded by a series of weak kings, during whose reign the power of Assyria declined, but in 745 the great Tiglath-pileser IV, mentioned in the Old Testament also under the name Pul, ascended the throne. He succeeded in reorganizing the resources of the empire and in rekindling its ambitions for conquest. This energetic king has left several inscriptions of much interest to the student of Old Testament history. In one of these, narrating an expedition against northern Syria about B. C. 738, he mentions a king, "Azriau of the land of Yaudi." It has been customary to identify this king with Azariah (Uzziah) of Judah. The contents speak against this identification, and since the inscriptions found in Zenjirli have established the existence in northern Syria of a state called Yaudi, perhaps the king mentioned in Tiglath-pileser's inscription was a ruler of this northern kingdom. In the annals which tell of his victory over Azriau of Yaudi he mentions Menahem of Samaria as one of the kings whose tribute he received. The same inscription, referring to events in 734 or 733, speaks of a victory over the House of Omri, and the assassination of the king Pekah, but the inscription is so fragmentary that the details are obscure. Fortunately, the same events are recorded in another inscription, which is in a better state of preservation, though it also has several gaps. After enumerating several cities which he captured in Palestine, among them Gaza, he continues: "The land of the dynasty of Omri . . . the whole of its inhabitants, their possessions to Assyria I deported. Pekah, their king, they slew, Hoshea to rule over them appointed. Ten talents of gold, a thousand talents of silver, I received as tribute." Ahaz of Judah is also mentioned in an inscription of Tiglath-pileser, as paying tribute, but it is not clear to what year this refers.

Tiglath-pileser died in 727, and was succeeded by Shalmaneser V, who in turn gave place in 722 to Sargon II. Shalmaneser is mentioned as the king who attacked the northern kingdom, and the Old Testament narrative leaves the impression that he was the king who finally captured the city of Samaria. The inscriptions show that it was Sargon who overcame the city soon after the beginning of his reign. In one of his inscriptions he calls himself, "the brave hero . . . who overthrew the House of Omri." In another he says: "Samaria I besieged, I took. 27,290 of its inhabitants I carried away; 50 chariots I gathered from them; the rest of them I permitted to retain their possessions. Over them I appointed my governor, and upon them I imposed the tribute of the former king." The annals of Sargon, which give an account of the events during his reign in chronological order, give the date of the capture of Samaria. After the introduction, he continues: "In the beginning of my reign and in the first year of my reign, . . . Samaria I besieged and took. . . . 27,290 inhabitants I carried away; 50 chariots as my royal portion I collected there. . . . I restored and made as it was before. . . . People from all countries, my captives, I settled there. My official I appointed as governor over them. Tribute and taxes like the Assyrian I imposed upon them."

After the destruction of the northern kingdom the life of the Hebrews became centered in Judah and Jerusalem. The fall of Samaria made an impression on the South that was remembered for some time. Nevertheless, the states along the eastern shore of the Mediterranean Sea bore impatiently the Assyrian yoke, and in most cities there arose a party which, relying on the promised help of Egypt, was eager to free itself from Assyria. That this party gained a foothold also in Jerusalem is seen from the prophecy in Isa. 20, in which the prophet warns the people against trusting in Egypt and rebelling against Assyria. In the same direction points an inscription of Sargon describing an expedition against Ashdod: "The people of Philistia, *Judah*, Edom, and Moab, dwelling beside the sea, bringing tribute and presents to Ashur my lord, were speaking treason. The people and their evil chiefs, to fight against me, to Pharaoh, king of Egypt, a prince who could not save them, their presents carried and besought his alliance." In all probability, Judah did not become involved seriously at this time. But the death of Sargon in 705 seems to have been a signal for revolt in many parts of the Assyrian empire. His son and successor, Sennacherib, gave these rebellions his immediate attention; until 702 he was kept busy in the East, but in that year he turned westward, and by 701 was ready to attack Judah. The campaign and the remarkable deliverance of Jerusalem on that occasion are recorded at length in 2 Kings 18, 19, and Isa. 36, 37. The account of the same campaign by the Assyrian king is, from the standpoint of Old Testament history, perhaps the most interesting historical inscription left by an Assyrian ruler. It is found in the so-called Taylor Cylinder,([15]) column 2, line 34, to column 3, line 41. The most interesting portion reads:

To the city of Ekron I went; the governors
[and] princes, who had committed a transgression, I killed and
bound their corpses on poles around the city.
The inhabitants of the city, who had committed sin and evil,
I counted as spoil; to the rest of them
who had committed no sin and wrong, who had
no guilt, I spoke peace. Padi
their king, I brought forth from the
city of Jerusalem; upon the throne of lordship over them
I placed him. The tribute of my lordship
I laid upon him. But Hezekiah
of Judah, who had not submitted to my yoke,
I besieged 46 of his strong cities, fortresses, and small cities
of their environs, without number, [and]
by the battering of rams and the assault of engines,
by the attack of foot soldiers, mines, breaches, and axes,
I besieged, I took them; 200,150 men, young [and] old, male
    and female, horses, mules, asses, camels, oxen
and sheep without number I brought out from them,
I counted them as spoil. [Hezekiah] himself I shut up like
    a caged bird in Jerusalem

his royal city; the walls I fortified
against him [and] whosoever came out of the gates of the
    city, I turned
back. His cities, which I had plundered, I separated from
    his land
and gave them to Mitinti, king of Ashdod,
to Padi, king of Ekron, and to Şil-Bel,
king of Gaza, and [thus] diminished his territory.
To the former tribute, paid yearly,
I added the tribute and presents of my lordship and
laid that upon him. Hezekiah himself
was overwhelmed by the fear of the brightness of my lordship;
the Arabians and his other faithful warriors
whom, as a defense for Jerusalem his royal city
he had brought in, fell into fear.
With 30 talents of gold [and] 800 talents of silver, precious
    stones,
gukhli daggassi (?), large lapis lazuli,
couches of ivory, thrones of ivory,
ivory, *usu* wood, box wood (?), of every kind, a heavy
    treasure,
and his daughters, his women of the palace,
the young men and young women, to Nineveh, the city of
    my lordship,
I caused to be brought after me, and he sent his ambassadors,
to give tribute and to pay homage.

These are, perhaps, the most important historical inscriptions illustrating specific events in
the history of Israel and Judah. There are, however, many more that make important, though
more or less indirect, contributions toward a better
understanding of Old Testament history. Just to
mention a few: Tirhaka of Egypt, who, temporarily
at least, interfered with the plans of the Assyrians,

appears several times in the inscriptions; the real significance of the events recorded in 2 Kings 20. 12ff., and Isa. 39, can be understood only in the light of the inscriptions; an interesting side-light is thrown by the inscriptions on the biblical account of Sennacherib's death. In one of the inscriptions of Esarhaddon, the son and successor of Sennacherib, we are told that among the twenty-two kings of the land of the Hittites who assisted him in his building enterprises was Manasseh, king of Judah. Ashurbanipal, the successor of Esarhaddon, includes Manasseh in a similar list. Though this king is not mentioned in the Old Testament under his Assyrian name, it is very probable that he is the king referred to in Ezra 4. 10, where it is said that the "great and noble Osnappar" brought Babylonians, Susanians, Elamites, and men of other nationalities to Samaria. The inscriptions do not throw much light upon the closing years of Judah's history, but we can understand the events in which Judah played a part better because the inscriptions set into clearer light the general history of Western Asia. The advance of the Scythians, the revival of Egypt in the seventh century, the fall of Nineveh, the rise of the Chaldean empire, which reached its highest glory under Nebuchadrezzar, the conqueror of Judah—all these are described in the inscriptions, or, at least, illuminated by them.

In a similar way the inscriptions, though not mentioning the Jewish exiles in Babylonia, illuminate the biblical records in many respects. Fortunately, also, the inscriptions furnish a good idea of the events leading to the downfall of Babylon, which resulted in the restoration of many exiles to Judah; and the restoration itself assumes a new significance in the light of the inscriptions; for the permission to return granted by Cyrus to the Jews is seen to be in accord with the general policy of the conqueror to secure the good-will of the peoples deported by the Babylonians by restoring them to their own homes. The historical situation of the age may suggest another reason for the kindly treatment of the Jews. It was inevitable that sooner or later Cyrus, or his successors, should come into conflict with Egypt. At such time it would be of immense value to him to have near the border of Egypt a nation upon whose fidelity and gratitude he could rely. Archæology has not thrown any direct light on the condition of the Jews in Palestine under the Persian rule. On the other hand, we know a great deal about conditions in Babylonia during that period, and within the past decade several important documents written on papyrus have been found in Egypt which furnish indisputable evidence that the island of Elephantine, opposite Assuan, a short distance north of the first cataract of the Nile, was the seat of a Jewish colony at least as early as the reign of Cambyses, king of Persia (B. C. 529–521).([16])

This concludes the survey of the archæological material of a historical nature. It is seen that during the period from the division of the kingdom subsequent to the death of Solomon to the reëstablishment of the Jews in Palestine after the exile the inscriptions furnish most interesting and instructive illustrations of events mentioned or alluded to in the Old Testament. As a result the history and also the prophecy of the Old Testament have been removed from the isolated position in which they previously seemed to stand. They are now seen to be connected by many links with the great movements taking place in the world without.

The question as to the bearing of the archæological historical records on the historical records of the Old Testament remains to be considered. This question was asked as soon as the contents of the inscriptions became known. The answers have varied greatly. On the one hand, it has been claimed that the Old Testament records are confirmed in every detail; on the other, those have not been wanting who claimed that the inscriptions discredit the Old Testament. Here, as in other investigations, the true conclusion can be reached only after a careful examination of all the facts in the case. In the study of the question there are several considerations and cautions which must not be lost sight of if we would reach a true estimate. Some of these cautions are suggested by the nature of the inscriptions.

In the first place, it must be remembered that most of the archæological material has come from lands outside of Palestine, and that the testimony is that of people not friendly to the Hebrews. We may expect, therefore, that at times personal bias may have colored the portrayal and caused the Hebrews to appear in a less favorable light than the facts would warrant, or that the events in which the Hebrews took part were described in a manner to make them favor the interests of the writers.

Again, not every period of Hebrew history is illuminated by the inscriptions. True, the earliest monuments found in Egypt and Babylonia antedate the birth of Jesus perhaps more than four thousand years; but it is not until the time of Ahab, king of Israel, that the important historical material begins. The references to Israel preceding the time of the Assyrian king, Shalmaneser III, c. B. C. 850, are few and more or less obscure. There is the monument of Shishak in the tenth century; but some are inclined to believe that the list of the cities alleged to have been conquered by Shishak was simply taken over by him from an earlier document, and that, therefore, it is of little or no historical value. Israel is mentioned in the inscription of Merneptah, but, as has been seen, the significance of the brief reference is obscure; there is nothing concerning the stay in Egypt, nothing concerning the patriarchs, and nothing concerning the earlier period that can in any way be connected with the historical records of the Old Testament.

Furthermore, to get at the true value of the evidence from the monuments we must distinguish between facts and inferences from the facts. This distinction, obvious as it seems, has not always been maintained even by eminent archæologists. For example, Professor Sayce, who is in just repute among Assyriologists, made a few years ago the statement: "The vindication of the reality of Menes [one of the early kings of Egypt] means the vindication also of the historical character of the Hebrew patriarchs." Surely, common sense says that facts proving the historicity of an early king of Egypt do not necessarily prove the historicity of men living many centuries later. Many similar illustrations might be given. Because bricks made without straw were found it has been claimed that every detail of the Old Testament narrative concerning the stay of Israel in Egypt was corroborated by archæology. The finding of the walls of royal palaces in Babylon furnished the claim that the story of the handwriting on the wall was established beyond doubt. The finding of images of deities has been interpreted as showing beyond a possibility of question the historicity of the narrative in Daniel concerning the image erected by Nebuchadrezzar, etc. There can easily be too much blind dependence on authority; an assumption of fact, upon the mere dictum of some presumably honest and competent scholar. About a generation ago a well-known investigator said, "Assyriology has its guesses and it has its accurate knowledge."([17]) These words might be expanded to include the whole field of archæology. Archæology has its facts, and it has its inferences. The two must not be confused.

Moreover, the possibility of inscribing lies upon clay tablets must not be overlooked. Sometimes it has been claimed, and that most absurdly, that because an inscription has been engraved upon imperishable stone or clay it has a superior value. But the mere fact of a record being inscribed on a tablet of clay, perishable or imperishable, gives it no superiority over one written on papyrus or parchment or paper. Clay tablets were to the civilization of the Euphrates valley what print paper is to us. We all know that paper is patient, else the daily papers would be of smaller size and many books would remain unwritten. The same is true of clay tablets. Clay tablets are patient. It was recognized long ago by Assyriologists that the so-called historical inscriptions are not all unbiased statements of objective facts. In many cases the chief purpose seems to have been the glorification of the king; victories are recorded with the greatest care, but no mention is made of defeats. For example: in one of the earliest inscriptions mentioning a king of Israel, Shalmaneser III, king of Assyria, claims a great victory over the Western allies in the battle of Karkar in 854; but, strange to say, the victory resulted in a rather hasty retreat of the Assyrian army. Another evidence of the "absolute reliability" of the historical tablets is offered by the inscriptions of the same king. In connection with the battle of Karkar, one inscription declares that the allies killed numbered 14,000; another, 20,500; while a third claims 25,000. We have, indeed, reason to say that "the evident uncertainty in the figures makes us doubt somewhat the clearness of the entire result. The claim of a great victory is almost certainly false."[18]

Once more: the translation of the inscriptions is not in every case beyond question. For example, in lines 7–9 of the Moabite Stone we read, according to the common translation, "Now Omri annexed all the land of Medeba, and Israel occupied it his days and half the days of his son, forty years." This rendering would imply that the period from the conquest under Omri to the end of the first half of Ahab's reign was forty years. The chronology of Kings gives as the total of the full reigns of the two kings only thirty-four years, while the above translation of the inscription would require about sixty—a serious discrepancy. Now, it is generally conceded that the chronology of the Bible cannot be accepted as final in all its details, and that it must be checked by the chronology of the inscriptions wherever that is possible. Yet before we can make use of the monumental testimony we should be sure of its exact meaning. In cases such as the one mentioned this certainty is absent, and we should move very slowly. Another translation of the passage has been proposed: "Omri conquered the whole land of Medeba and held it in possession as long as he reigned and during half of my reign his son, in all forty years; but yet in my reign Chemosh recovered it."[19] This translation would bring the total of the two reigns to about forty years, and thus the chronological difficulty apparently offered by 2 Kings 3 would be removed.

The five considerations to which attention has been called must be observed if we would understand rightly the bearing of the monuments on the Old Testament, when viewed from the standpoint of the inscriptions. Attention must now be called to certain considerations touching

primarily the Old Testament that must be regarded in forming an estimate of the value of
its historical records.

We must remember, for example, that the purpose of the Old Testament is essentially and pre-
dominatingly religious. This is recognized by the
Jews, for they do not call any of the so-called
historical books by that name. The five books
of the Pentateuch they designate as Law, because
in these books practically all Hebrew legislation
is embodied. Joshua, Judges, Samuel, Kings, they
include in the list of prophetic books, because
they recognize the essentially prophetic purpose
of the authors. The other books belong to the
third division of the Jewish canon, called the
Writings. Concerning the books of Kings, which
are the principal historical books of the Old
Testament, it has been truly said: "Kings, by
virtue of its contents, belongs as much to the
prophetical books as to the historical. It is not
a continuous chronicle; it is a book of prophetic
teaching in which sometimes history, sometimes
story, is employed as the vehicle of teaching. It
enforces the principle that God is the controlling
power and sin the disturbing force in the entire
history of men and nations.[20] In a similar
manner the religious purpose predominates in the
other Old Testament historical books. They do
not pretend to give a complete history even of

the Hebrew people. The writers embodied only
such historical material as was thought to illustrate
the self-revelation of God in the history of individuals and of the nation, or to bear in some
marked way upon the coming of the kingdom of
God. A modern secular historian is disappointed
at many omissions which would be unpardonable
in a strictly historical production. Now, it is
readily seen that the religious purpose may be
served, and the didactic value of the narrative
may remain, even though historical inaccuracies
in details should be discovered.

Another fact to be remembered is the possible
difference in the viewpoint of several narrators of
one and the same event. In sacred, as in secular
history, the viewpoint of the author determines
to a considerable extent the character of the
narrative. For example: the delineation of the
events of the Civil War will not be the same in
official documents, in a secular history, in a church
history, or in a work containing personal memoirs.
Still other differences might be seen in narratives
confined to special incidents. Such differences in
viewpoint may be noticed also among the writers
of the Old Testament historical books. Broadly
speaking, part of the historical literature of the
Old Testament is due to prophetic activity, part
to priestly activity. In writing history the
prophets, with their broad interest in all the

affairs of the nation, resemble the modern secular historian. They portray events more objectively than the priests, hence they are more reliable. The priestly writers resemble the modern ecclesiastical historian, who judges everyone and everything according to their attitude toward the peculiar religious conceptions he represents. The Old Testament contains also some personal memoirs (in Ezra and Nehemiah) and some narratives of special incidents (Ruth, Esther), while the historical books in their present form embody also what may have been official documents.

Moreover, in estimating the reliability of the Old Testament historical books we must not overlook certain unconscious references and indications which show that the authors exercised considerable care in producing the books. In the first place, historical statements appear to have been preserved with considerable care, at least so far as the substance is concerned. This may be seen from the retention of parallel narratives of the same events, without attempts at harmonizing minor disagreements. In the second place, history was written with some discrimination. This is evident especially in Kings, where the several degrees in which certain of the kings departed from the legitimate religion of Israel are carefully indicated. A clear distinction is made between the relatively pious kings, who simply did not remove the high places (1 Kings 15. 14; 2 Kings 12. 3) and those who, in defiance of a fundamental principle (Exod. 20. 4, 5), desired to represent the spiritual God of Israel in images that would appeal to the senses (1 Kings 12. 28, 29; 14. 16, etc.), and those who, in defiance of the first requirement of the Decalogue (Exod. 20. 3), served other gods (1 Kings 16. 31–33; 18. 22, etc.). Once more: in the Old Testament records we find evidence of the historical consciousness of ancient Israel resting upon a very sure foundation. The Mosaic age was regarded as the supreme crisis in the national history. Moses was the great hero; yet his grandeur was not able to extinguish the consciousness of the glory of the pre-Mosaic period. Throughout the entire literature Abraham and Jacob and Joseph are also connected with the beginnings of the Hebrew nation and with the beginning of the religious mission of the people. The memory of the pre-Mosaic period seems indeed to have been securely founded.

What, then, are the results of this comparative study ? The Old Testament world has become a new world. Dark regions were Egypt, Assyria, Elam, and other countries mentioned in the Old Testament before the explorers and excavators entered these lands. Now it is comparatively easy to trace with considerable accuracy the boundaries of empires that existed in the first and second millenniums B. C. In addition, we can fix with certainty the sites of some Old Testament cities whose location was previously unknown and, in some cases, whose very existence had been doubted. The topography of cities like Nineveh, Nippur, and Babylon has become quite definitely fixed.

The historical gains are even more remarkable. Whole nations have been resurrected. What did we know a century ago of Elam? Nothing but the name. What of Assyria? Only a few traditions, sometimes untrustworthy, preserved by classical writers, and the statements of the Bible, some of which were unintelligible because of their fragmentary character. Now these and other nations pass one after the other in review, great and powerful in all their ancient glory. And, almost every day, new light is thrown on these early centuries. Only a few years ago it was thought that Assyrian history, as distinct from that of Babylon, began about B. C. 1800; now we know the names of many rulers who lived generations and centuries before that date.

The chronological gains are especially important. It is generally admitted that Hebrew chronology is not always reliable, and various expedients have been resorted to to remove the difficulties. It was very gratifying, therefore, to discover that the chronological system of the Assyrians was

more precise. Among the inscriptions are especially three classes of public records in which the
occurrences are carefully dated: (1) Records of
the reigns of certain kings in which their activities
are carefully arranged in chronological order;
(2) business tablets in which transactions are
definitely dated; and (3) the so-called eponym
lists. According to Assyrian custom, each year
was named after a prominent official. Lists of
these were carefully made and kept, and, fortunately, large fragments of them have been
preserved. Two recensions of these eponym lists
have come down. In one only the names of
the years are given; in the other references to
important events are added to the names. If,
now, any one of these events can be dated, it
becomes possible to trace the dates designated by
the names on either side of the one whose date
is first determined. By means of these lists and
the other records the Assyrian chronology can be
definitely fixed from about B. C. 900 on. This,
in turn, enables us to bring order into the chaos
of Hebrew chronology during the most important
period of the nation's existence.

When we think of these and other gains, not
the least of which is the discovery of the contemporaneous documents, the absence of which
was at one time made the basis for the rejection
of many statements found exclusively in the Old

Testament, we may gratefully receive this new light and rejoice in the advance in Bible knowledge made possible through the excavations. What, now, is the general bearing of these discoveries on the trustworthiness of the Old Testament?

In the first place, it is well to remember that for many periods of Hebrew history we are still entirely dependent on the Old Testament for direct information. For example, Professor Clay's claim concerning the patriarchal age, that "the increase of knowledge gained through the inscriptions of this period has in every instance dissolved conclusions arrived at by those critics who maintain that the patriarchs are not to be regarded as historical,"[21] is not justified by the facts. In reality, no incident in the patriarchal story is referred to in any of the inscriptions read thus far. On the other hand, the age of the patriarchs has been wonderfully illuminated. "Formerly the world in which the patriarchs moved seemed to be almost empty; now we see it filled with embassies, armies, busy cities, and long lines of traders passing to and fro between one center of civilization and another; but amid all that crowded life we peer in vain for any trace of the fathers of the Hebrews; we listen in vain for any mention of their names; this is the whole change archæology has wrought: it has given us an atmosphere and a background for the stories of Genesis; it is

unable to recall or certify their heroes."[22] All
that can be said in this, as in other cases, is, that
archæology, by furnishing a broad historical background, has established the possibility of the
principal events recorded in the biblical narratives
being correct. It is silent concerning the events
themselves, and, therefore, neither confirms nor
discredits them.

A few cases there are, especially in connection
with questions of chronology, where archæology
has modified and corrected biblical statements.
According to the inscriptions of Tiglath-pileser,
for example, Menahem of Israel paid tribute to
the Assyrian king in B. C. 738, and there is reason
for believing that this tribute was paid near the
beginning of Menahem's reign for the purpose of
securing the good will of Assyria. In 734 or 733
Pekah is said to have been slain and to have
been succeeded by Hoshea. Now, according to the
Old Testament, Menahem reigned ten years; his
son, Pekahiah, two years, and Pekah twenty
years, a total of thirty-two years. Even if we
assume that the tribute was paid by Menahem
during his last year—which is not at all likely—
there would remain twenty-two years to be provided for between 738 and 734 or 733. Evidently,
the Old Testament figures are too high. A
similar case is found in connection with events
that took place only a few years later. In 2 Kings

18. 10 the statement is found that Samaria was taken in the sixth year of Hezekiah, king of Judah. Then, verse 13 states that in the fourteenth year of Hezekiah, Sennacherib, king of Assyria, came against Jerusalem. The date of the capture of Samaria is definitely fixed by the Assyrian inscriptions. The city fell either in the closing days of B. C. 722 or the opening days of B. C. 721. Assuming that it was 722, the fourteenth year of Hezekiah would be 714. But Sennacherib did not become king until 705, and the attack upon Jerusalem was not made until 701. Here, again, the biblical account seems to be inaccurate.

In many other cases, however, remarkable confirmations are seen. There are many persons and events mentioned in the Old Testament which are referred to also in the inscriptions. Think of the long list of Babylonian and Assyrian kings named in the Old Testament; Amraphel, king of Shinar, at one time considered a mythical figure, is shown to have been one of the greatest generals, wisest administrators, and fairest lawgivers among the early kings of Babylon. Sargon, whose very existence was once doubted, has in defiance risen from the dust. In these and numerous other cases, especially from the ninth century onward—as may be seen from a comparison of the inscriptions quoted above with the corresponding portions of the Old Testament—the archæological records furnish striking confirmations of the Old Testament narratives. To sum up this entire inquiry: It must be apparent to every unbiased student that the monuments, when read intelligently, neither set aside nor discredit the Old Testament documents. On the contrary, they prove their substantial accuracy. They may at times modify them, especially in questions of chronology; but they more frequently corroborate than impugn; thus they offer their services not as a substitute but as a supplement, by the aid of which we may study from without the history of the Hebrew people.

NOTES ON CHAPTER IV

(¹) An excellent account of the explorations and excavations in Babylonia and Assyria, and of the decipherment of the inscriptions is found in R. W. Rogers, A History of Babylonia and Assyria, Vol. I, Chapters I—VIII; compare also H. V. Hilprecht, Explorations in Bible Lands during the Nineteenth Century, Part I.

(²) Preliminary reports of the results of the German excavations are given from time to time in the Mitteilungen der Deutschen Orient Gesellschaft.

(³) G. Steindorff, Excavations in Egypt, in H. V. Hilprecht, Explorations in Bible Lands, pp. 623–690.

(⁴) Opening words of I. Benzinger, Researches in Palestine, in Hilprecht, Explorations, pp. 579–622. A very complete discussion of explorations and excavations in Palestine may be found in F. Jones Bliss, Development of Palestine Exploration. The progress of the excavations is reported in the Quarterly Statement of the Palestine Exploration Fund.

(^{5}) Opening words of the first lecture on "Babel and Bible."

(^{6}) S. R. Driver, The Book of Genesis, p. xlviii.

(^{7}) A. T. Clay, Light on the Old Testament from Babel, Chapter XI.

(^{8}) The Chronology of the Old Testament, p. 97.

(^{9}) Egypt and Israel, p. 35. Breasted also seems to think that the Israelites defeated by Merneptah had no direct connection with those who suffered in Egypt, A History of Egypt, p. 466; compare p. 410.

(^{10}) The Expositor, 1908, p. 199.

(^{11}) J. C. Ball, Light from the East, pp. 131, 132.

(^{12}) W. H. Bennett, The Moabite Stone; Hastings, Dictionary of the Bible, art., "Moab, Moabites."

(^{13}) Most of the inscriptions from this period on are found in D. G. Hogarth, Authority and Archæology, Part I—Hebrew Authority, by S. R. Driver. See also T. G. Pinches, The Old Testament in the Light of the Historical Records and Legends of Assyria and Babylonia; A. T. Clay, Light on the Old Testament from Babel; A. Jeremias, The Old Testament in the Light of the Ancient Orient; R. F. Harper, Assyrian and Babylonian Literature; S. R. Driver, Modern Research as Illustrating the Bible. The most recent and most complete collection of cuneiform inscriptions throwing light on Old Testament religion and history is contained in R. W. Rogers, Cuneiform Parallels to the Old Testament, which appeared after this book had gone to press.

(^{14}) Formerly called Shalmaneser II; see Expository Times, February, 1912, p. 238.

(^{15}) A translation of the entire inscription by R. W. Rogers is found in Records of the Past, New Series, Vol. VI, pp. 80ff. These Records of the Past contain translations of the more important ancient inscriptions.

(¹⁶) The most important of these papyri is translated in the Biblical World, June, 1908, pp. 448ff.

(¹⁷) Francis Brown, Assyriology—Its Use and Abuse in Old Testament Study, p. 3.

(¹⁸) R. W. Rogers, History of Babylonia and Assyria, Vol. II, p. 80.

(¹⁹) Encyclopedia Biblica, Vol. I, col. 792, Note.

(²⁰) E. W. Barnes, The First Book of Kings, p. xxxiii.

(²¹) A. T. Clay, Light on the Old Testament from Babel, p. 143.

(²²) S. R. Driver, The Book of Genesis, p. liii, quoted in part from G. A. Smith, Modern Criticism and the Preaching of the Old Testament, p. 101.

CHAPTER V

The Old Testament and Comparative Religion

The present is an era of comparative study. We no longer study subjects by themselves, but compare them with correlated experiences and phenomena. "In the sphere of language study we have the science of comparative philology. Language is compared with language. By means of this comparison we have found that there are groups of languages closely related to one another; and, comparing these groups with one another, we have discovered certain universal laws of language. Comparing further the languages within each group, we ascertain the laws common to that group. By such comparison a flood of light has been thrown on language. We know Greek and Latin and Hebrew to-day as our predecessors did not know them."[1] The same principle of comparison is now applied to the study of history, of literature, of philosophy, of ethics, and of religion, including the literature and religion of the Hebrews. Men are laying to-day the entire Hebrew literature, history, and religion alongside of the literatures, histories, and religions of other nations, testing them by the same methods and applying to them the same rules.

What should be the attitude of the Christian toward this method of study? When the science of comparative philology first asserted itself many good Christians set themselves against it, because one of its claims was that Hebrew is not the original language given by God to men. Comparative philology has won its way, and Bible students are truly grateful for the light it has shed upon sacred scripture. When the comparative study of the Scriptures was first advocated there were many timid souls who felt that this method of study was an attack upon the Bible, which could only issue in such an overturning of belief that the Church would remain helpless with a worthless Bible. Hence they set themselves with all their might against the new study as an enemy of Christianity. Is this the proper attitude? In the first place, it is well to remember that the Bible has withstood all attacks for thousands of years. Its great river of truth has flowed serenely on, watering the whole earth with its life-giving streams, and refusing to be dammed up by any foe. Surely, history teaches that there need be no fear that any new method of study will bring about an end of the Bible's reign. On the other hand, history teaches the folly of resisting the progress of science along any line of investigation.

True science will win its way just as surely as the teaching of the Bible will win its way into the hearts of men. Hence it would seem the part of wisdom to encourage rather than to discourage the efforts of the comparative student of the Old Testament.

As a matter of fact, we cannot do anything else unless we would stultify ourselves. We have said to the adherents of every other religion: "You say your sacred books are divine, prove it; lay your books open before the· jury of the world, let the critics scrutinize them, analyze them, criticize them, according to the canons of modern criticism by which they criticize all books." And can we refuse to open our Bible before the jury of the world and bid it scrutinize, analyze, and criticize it according to the same canons which it applies to the Veda, the Koran, and other so-called holy books? Would such an attitude be fair? If we believe that the Bible is different from the sacred books of other nations, that it stands on a far higher plane, unique, needing no concealment and no bolstering up with traditions and doctrines— if that is our faith, then let us lay it down open before the world and challenge men to read it, study it, and compare it with all the sacred literatures of the world. The man who really believes in the inspiration of the Bible ought not to be afraid of such a test. He may rest assured that the comparative study of biblical literature and biblical religion will prove one of the things that work together for good to all those who have a living faith in God.

An exhaustive discussion of the subject of this chapter would involve a study of all the great historical religions, known better to-day than ever before, and a comparison of them with the religion of the Old Testament. This, however, could not be done satisfactorily within the limits of a single chapter. It seems, therefore, advisable to confine the investigation to the religious beliefs, practices, and institutions of the nations with whom the Hebrews came into more or less close contact, such as the Babylonians, Assyrians, and Egyptians. Political contact, which was common between these nations and the Hebrews, might furnish occasions for exerting influence in the realms of religion, law, and other elements of civilization. "When alien races and diverse faiths confronted each other it might not always be the cause of war, but it was always the occasion of psychical conflict."[2] Since the knowledge of the religions of the nations named has been supplied very largely through archæological labors, this inquiry is simply one phase of the broader question as to the bearing of archæology upon the Old Testament; more especially, the bearing of the archæological material of a religious and ethical nature upon the uniqueness and permanent significance of the Old Testament religion.

The importance of this study is suggested in the following quotation from a prominent Assyriologist, Hugo Winckler: "We come in the end to this, that we can distinguish only two views of the world which the human race has known in its historical development: the old Babylonian, and the modern empirical naturalistic, which is still in process of development and is yet struggling with the old one in many departments of life."[3] To avoid misunderstanding respecting the extent of the Babylonian influence, he adds, "The view of the world and religion are *one* for the ancient Oriental."[3]   In this statement Winckler robs the Old Testament religion of all originality; he considers it simply a natural development of the Babylonian religion. Friedrich Delitzsch, in his lectures on "Babel and Bible,"[4] expresses the same idea in a slightly modified form and attempts to show the predominance of Babylonian thought in the Hebrew conception of the origin of the world, the Fall, the Flood, life after death, angels, demons, the devil, the Sabbath, a large part of the sacrificial cult, the directions concerning the priesthood, the name and worship of Jehovah, and even in the monotheistic conception of Deity. How much truth is there in these claims? Or, to put the question in another form, If the religious ideas expressed in the Old Testament have parallels among nations commonly called heathen, and if these extra-biblical ideas cannot be explained as dependent on the Bible, does it follow that the ideas of the Bible are appropriated from these nations, and if so, what becomes of the uniqueness, the sacredness, the inspiration of the Old Testament? In order to answer the question adequately it is necessary to consider in detail the most important phases of the religious ideas of the Hebrews on the one hand, and of the nations with whom the Hebrews came in contact on the other.

Fundamental to all religious thinking is the conception of Deity. The origin of the Babylonian conception of Deity, which shows more striking similarities to the ideas of the Old Testament than do the conceptions of the other nations above mentioned, belongs to a period of which little or nothing is known. But there are indications that a fundamental aspect of the earliest religion of the country was animism, that is, the belief that every object was possessed and animated by a spirit. "Life was the only force known to man which explained motion, and, conversely, motion was the sign and manifestation of life. The arrow which sped through the air, or the rock which fell from the cliff, did so in virtue of their possessing life, or because the motive force of life lay in some way or other behind them. The stars, which slowly moved through the sky, and the sun, which rose and set day by day, were living beings. It was life which gave them the power of movement as it gave the power of movement to man himself, and the animals by whom he was surrounded."(⁵) Besides this belief in animism, the Babylonian religion shows evidences of a belief in ghosts that were related to the world of the dead. These ghosts were thought to exercise an evil influence upon men and could be cast out only by the use of incantations.

But, while these elements belonged to the early religion, Babylonian religion as it actually meets us even in the earliest inscriptions has reached a higher stage of development. There appear many local deities; every center of human habitation had its special patron deity; for example, Babylon was the city of Marduk; Nippur, of Enlil; Ur, of Sin; Sippara, of Shamash; Cuthah, of Nergal; Asshur, of Ashur; etc. These deities are usually associated with natural phenomena; foremost among them stand the sun and the moon; but by the side of these many other natural objects or forces were personified and deified.

It is probable that in the beginning, as the result of limited observation and speculation, the number of gods in the Babylonian pantheon was relatively small. However, in the course of time, they became greatly multiplied as the result of a wider observation of the phenomena of nature political changes, and theological speculation. Over against this tendency to multiply deities there shows itself, in the course of the centuries, a tendency to diminish the number of gods, and in the end comparatively few remain, until in the late Babylonian period the worship seems to have been confined chiefly to Marduk, Nabu, Sin, Shamash, and Ishtar. Some of the great thinkers of Babylonia seem to have gone even so far as to consider the various deities manifestation of the one god Marduk. There is in existence a tablet of the Neo-Babylonian period which states that Marduk is called Ninib as the possessor of power, Nergal as lord of battle, Bel as possessor of dominion, Nabu as lord of business, Sin as the illuminator of the night, Shamash as the lord of right, Addu as the lord of rain, etc.([6]) It is seen, then, that monotheistic tendencies are not absent from the Babylonian religion. But they never go beyond the realm of speculation. "The Babylonians, with all their wonderful gifts, were never able to conceive of one god, of one god alone, of one god whose very existence makes logically impossible the existence of any other deity. Monotheism transcends the spiritual grasp of the Babylonian mind."([7]) In the words of Delitzsch, "Notwithstanding all this, however, and despite the fact that many liberal and enlightened minds openly advocated the doctrine that Nergal and Nebo, that the moon-god and the sun-god, the god of thunder, Ramman, and all the rest of the Babylonian pantheon, were one in Marduk, the god of light, still polytheism, gross polytheism, remained for three thousand years the Babylonian state religion—a sad and significant warning against the indolence of men and races in matters of religion, and against the colossal power which may be acquired by a strongly organized priesthood based upon it."([8])

Even the most spiritual expressions of the Babylonian religion, the so-called penitential psalms, bear witness to the fact that the writers continued to worship many deities. In one of the most spiritual of these psalms, the psalmist prays:

> That the heart anger of my lord be appeased,
> A god unknown to me be appeased,
> A goddess unknown to me be appeased,
> A known and unknown god be appeased,
> A known and unknown goddess be appeased,
> That the heart of my god be appeased,
> The heart of my goddess be appeased,
> God and goddess, known and unknown, be appeased.([9])

Some of the hymns and prayers addressed to certain deities read almost as if the authors were monotheists. But this is due simply to the fact that just at the time they are interested in the power or splendor or favor of a specific deity. Again and again the fact that they believe in the existence of other deities, and in their duty to pay homage to different deities, crops out. At no period of the religious history of Babylonia is there any indication of a clear and well-defined monotheism.

In Egypt also a tendency toward monotheism manifested itself, especially during the reign of Amenophis IV, soon after B. C. 1400,([10]) that is, during the period when the Hebrews were in Egypt. He tried to do away with the worship of many deities and to establish as the one supreme deity the orb of the sun; but after the death of Amenophis, who was considered a heretic, the new cult disappeared without exerting any noticeable influence on Egyptian religion. There certainly is no evidence that either the Babylonian or the Egyptian monotheistic tendencies influenced in any direct way the development of Israel's religion.

Turning now to the religion of the Old Testament, we soon discover that Hebrew religion, including the conception of Deity, passed through various stages of development, the earliest of these belonging to the period before Moses. The first thing to be noted about this period is that, in spite of the close relation of the ancient Hebrews with Babylon, the early Hebrew conception of Deity does not seem to have been influenced in any marked manner by that of Babylonia; nor is there any indication of Egyptian influence. On the other hand, the oldest Hebrew conceptions show marked similarities with the religion of their nomadic neighbors, as reflected, for example, in the oldest traditions of the Arab tribes. This does not mean that an indirect influence may not have been exerted by Babylon; indeed, the absence of such influence would be very strange in view of the fact that, according to Hebrew tradition, the truth of which cannot be doubted, the ancestors of the Hebrews came from Babylonia, from the city of Ur, the principal center of the worship of the Babylonian moon-god, Sin.

The results of modern investigations into the nature of early Hebrew religion may be briefly stated as follows: Like the early Babylonian religion, the religion of Israel passed through a stage of animism. In one form this is the belief in the activity of the spirits of recently deceased relatives. But this becomes a religion only when it leads to the worship of the departed, that is, ancestor worship, of which there is no definite indication in the biblical material at our command. But there is a form of animism of which there are traces in Israel as in Babylonia, namely, the worship of spirits that were believed to be the inhabitants and possessors of certain objects and places, like trees, stones, springs, which thereby assumed a sacred character. To this form of

religion the name "polydemonism," which means
the worship of many demons, is ordinarily given.
Demon, however, is to be understood here, not
in the sense of evil spirit, but simply a divine
being of an inferior order. As illustrations of this
belief, attention may be called to the sacred stone,
Bethel, which gave the locality its name, "House
of God" (Gen. 28. 19), or to the sacred oracular
tree at Shechem (Gen. 12. 6; Deut. 11. 30), or to
the sacred wells at Kadesh (Gen. 14. 7) and
Beersheba (Gen. 21. 28–33). In general, it may
be said that during the pre-Mosaic period the
religion of Israel, whatever may have been true of
isolated individuals, was not essentially different
from the religious conceptions of the people with
which we have become better acquainted through
modern exploration and excavation.([11])

Another and very different conception appears
from the time of the exodus on. The most
striking feature of this new conception is that the
Israelites now worship one God, whom they consider their own peculiar Deity, while they look
upon themselves as his own peculiar people. True,
the earlier conceptions did not disappear entirely
or immediately; but for the religious leaders
there was but one God who had a right to demand
Israel's loyalty. Jehovah, or Yahweh, was the
name of this God, and the religious watchword
was, "Jehovah, the God of Israel; Israel the people

of Jehovah." Now archæology has shown the name "Yahweh" to have been used as a divine name long before the time of the exodus; but archæology has also shown that the conception of the nature and character of Yahweh held by the religious leaders of the Hebrews from the time of Moses on is peculiar to them. Says R. W. Rogers, "There can, therefore, be no escape from the conclusion that the divine name 'Yahweh' is not a peculiar possession of the Hebrews."[12] Then he continues: "At first sight this may seem like a startling robbery of Israel, this taking away from her the divine name 'Yahweh' as an exclusive possession, but it is not so. Yahweh himself is not taken away: he remains the priceless possession, the chief glory of Israel. It is only the name that is shown to be widespread. And the name matters little. The great question is, What does this name convey? What is its theological content? The name came to Israel from the outside; but into that vessel a long line of prophets from Moses onward poured such a flood of attributes as never a priest in all western Asia from Babylonia to the sea ever dreamed of in his highest moments of spiritual insight. In this name and through Israel's history God chose to reveal himself to Israel, and by Israel to the world. Therein lies the supreme and lonesome superiority of Israel over Babylonia."[13]

Archæology has revealed the pantheon of Babylonia and Assyria; the inscriptions have also set in a clear light the nature and character of the gods as conceived by their worshipers. For example, the gods are looked upon as a part of the process of creation, as may be seen from the opening lines of the story of Creation:([14])

> When no one of the gods had been called into being,
> And none bore a name, and no destinies were fixed.
> Then were created the gods in the midst of heaven.

An idea of the character of these deities may be gathered from the description of a heavenly banquet scene in the same poem:

> They made ready the feast, at the banquet [they sat],
> They ate bread, they mingled the wine.
> The sweet drink made them drunken . .
> By drinking they were drunken, their bodies were filled.
> They shouted aloud, their heart was exalted,
> Then for Marduk, their avenger, did they decree destiny.

Certainly, not all the religious thinkers of Babylonia held these low conceptions. In some of their prayers and hymns they rise to lofty spiritual and ethical conceptions which compare quite favorably with expressions found in the Old Testament. In a hymn addressed to Shamash, the sun-god, are found these lines:

Who plans evil—his horn thou dost destroy,
Whoever in fixing boundaries annuls rights.
The unjust judge thou restrainest with force.

Whoever accepts a bribe, who does not judge justly—on him
   thou imposest sin.
But he who does not accept a bribe, who has a care for the
   oppressed,
To him Shamash is gracious, his life he prolongs.
The judge who renders a just decision
Shall end in a palace, the place of princes shall be his dwelling.
   . . . .
The seed of those who act unjustly shall not flourish.
What their mouth declares in thy presence
Thou shalt burn it up, what they purpose wilt thou annul.
Thou knowest their transgressions; the declaration of the
   wicked thou dost cast aside.
Every one wherever he may be is in thy care.
Thou directest their judgments, the imprisoned dost thou
   liberate.
Thou hearest, O Shamash, petition, prayer, and appeal,
Humility, prostration, petitioning, and reverence.
With loud voice the unfortunate one cries to thee.
The weak, the exhausted, the oppressed, the lowly,
Mother, wife, maid appeal to thee,
He who is removed from his family, he that dwelleth far from
   his city.([15])

Far be it from the writer to rob the religion of
Babylonia of any of its glory. Nevertheless, he
ventures to assert without any fear of contradic-
tion that we may search the pantheon of Babylon,
from one end to the other, and we shall not find
one god who in nature and character can compare
with the Jehovah of Israel as proclaimed by the
great prophets and glorified by the sweet singers
of the nation, a God "merciful and gracious, slow
to anger, and abundant in loving-kindness and
truth." We may well speak of a "great gulf,

which is fixed between primitive Semitic conceptions of God and the noble spiritual views of him set forth under divine illumination by Isaiah."([16]) It is due to this fundamental difference in the conception of the nature and character of Deity that the religion of Israel became "a living and ethical power, growing and increasing until Jesus, greatest of the prophets, completed the message of his predecessors," and Christianity was born.

From the conception of Deity we may pass to a brief consideration of religious institutions and beliefs. One of the most important results of recent archæological discoveries has been to show that many of the religious rites, customs, and institutions of Babylonia and Assyria, as also of Egypt, resemble closely those assigned in the Old Testament to the Hebrews. This cannot appear strange when we remember that Israel was a branch of the great Semitic race, which was, at the time of its separation from the common stock, in possession of many of the common Semitic notions and practices. It would have been impossible to rid the Israelite consciousness of all of these; therefore the religious leaders of the Hebrews took the better way of retaining the familiar forms and pouring into them a new, higher, and more spiritual significance.

One of the earliest religious institutions recognized in the Old Testament is the Sabbath. The very fact that it is mentioned in the story of creation shows that, whatever the reason for its observance among the Hebrews, it was recognized as a very ancient institution. Has archæology thrown any light on the origin of the Sabbath day?([17])   In his first lecture on "Babel and Bible," Delitzsch answers the question in these words: "There can therefore be scarcely the shadow of a doubt that in the last resort we are indebted to this ancient nation on the banks of the Euphrates and the Tigris for the plenitude of blessings that flows from our day of Sabbath, or Sunday, rest."([18]) This statement was soon criticized, because it seemed to give too much credit to the Babylonians, and Delitzsch later modified the statement and claimed, simply, that the Hebrew Sabbath ultimately is rooted in a Babylonian institution.([19]) No exception can be taken to this putting of the claim.

What are the facts in the case?   (1) The Babylonians observed in a peculiar way the seventh, fourteenth, twenty-first, and twenty-eighth days of the month, that is, the days on which the moon entered a new phase. They also observed the nineteenth day of the month, which was the forty-ninth day from the beginning of the preceding month. These days were considered unlucky days, on which certain actions had to be avoided, at least by important personages, like the king, priest, and physician. The prohibition reads: "The shepherd (king) of the great nations shall not eat roasted nor smoked meat, not change his garment, not put on white raiment, not offer sacrifice; the king shall not mount his chariot, as ruler not pronounce judgment; the priest shall not give oracles in the secret place; the physician shall not lay his hand on the sick, the day being inauspicious for any affair whatever." The Babylonians evidently observed these days by at least partial cessation of work, because nothing would prosper anyway on those days. In contrast, it may be well to notice that in the Sabbath observance among the early Hebrews the humanitarian element played a prominent part. (2) The name *Sha-bat-tu* has been found in the inscriptions as an interpretation of the phrase, *um nuḫ libbi*, which means, a day for appeasing the heart (of the deity). It would seem, therefore, that the Babylonian Sabbath was intended to be a day of atonement or supplication, which might imply cessation of ordinary labor, especially since the word *Sha-bat-tu* may be identical in meaning with *gamaru*, to complete or finish, which leads naturally to the idea of rest, because the work is completed. (3) There is no definite evidence that the five days mentioned were called *Sha-bat-tu;* the name is given rather to the fifteenth day of the month, which is the day of the full moon.

In the light of these facts it is not improbable that there is some connection between the Hebrew Sabbath and certain special days among the Babylonians; but, as in other cases, the Hebrews have given to the adopted institution a new significance. Some of the changes introduced by the Hebrews are: (a) The Hebrews observed every seventh day without regard for the month or the year. The Babylonians observed the seventh, fourteenth, twenty-first, and twenty-eighth days of each month. (b) The motive underlying the observance among the two people differs. The earliest Hebrew legislation (Exod. 23. 12) would seem to indicate that humanitarian considerations are responsible for Sabbath observance, not religious superstition. (c) The Sabbath law of the Hebrews was binding on all. According to our present knowledge, among the Babylonians only the leaders appear to have been affected.

The Babylonians, Egyptians, and other ancient peoples had in addition to the Sabbath numerous other festivals, and it is not improbable that some of the Hebrew festivals are connected with these, though the exact relation is not yet determined.

Archæology has thrown much light on the complicated ceremonial system of the Old Testament, though it is an exaggeration to say that, "if we want to trace the origin of the late Jewish ceremonial of the Priest Code, we must look for

it in the cuneiform ritual texts of the Babylonians."[20]   Attention may be called here to a
few of the more marked similarities between the
Hebrew and Babylonian systems.[21]   (1) The
Babylonian temple closely resembled the temple
of Solomon. Both had two courts, chambers for
the priests, the sanctuary, and the Holy of holies.
Externally, both were mere rectangular boxes,
without much architectural beauty or variety of
design. It was only in the possession of a tower
that the Babylonian temple differed from the
Hebrew, a difference due to a difference in the
conception of Deity. The temples agreed even
in the details of their furniture: the two altars of
the Babylonian sanctuary are found again in the
temple of Jerusalem; so also the mercy seat and
the table of showbread. The bronze sea of
Solomon was modeled after a Babylonian original.
The twin pillars, which Solomon erected in the
porch of the temple, have their counterparts in
Babylonian sanctuaries. Even the sacred ark
seems to have had a Babylonian origin, though
some would trace it to Egypt.   (2) Every great
sanctuary had its chief priest. Under him was a
large number of subordinate priests and temple
ministers, such as sacrificers, pourers of libations,
anointers with oil, bakers, chanters, wailers, etc.
Connected with the sanctuaries were also the
prophets, augurs, soothsayers, necromancers, etc.

Though not all these classes of religious workers are found in connection with the Jewish sanctuaries, the chief priest and his subordinates are found there as well as in Babylon. (3) Similarities in the details of the sacrificial system may be noted. Libations were poured out before the deities, consisting originally, probably, of pure water, to which was subsequently added wine, made either from the palm or the vine. All the first-fruits of the cultivated land were offered to the god; milk and butter and oil, dates and vegetables were given in abundance. So too were spices and incense, brought from the southern coast of Arabia, the corn that was grown in the fields, garlic and other herbs from the garden, and honey from the hive. Annual sacrifices were not forgotten. Oxen and calves, sheep and lambs, goats and kids, fish and certain kinds of birds, were slain upon the altar. There are traces of human sacrifice, but, as among the Hebrews, the practice disappeared at an early date. "Babylonia," says Sayce, "was the inventor of the tithe,"[22] which was paid by all classes, even the king. One of the last acts recorded of the crown prince, Belshazzar, is the payment of a tithe, forty-seven shekels in amount, due from his sister to the temple of the sun-god at Sippara. The daily sacrifice was a fixed custom. Several of the technical terms of the Old Testament are found also in Assyrian. For example: *torah*, law, has its counterpart in the Assyrian *tertu;* the biblical *kipper*, atonement, is the Assyrian *kuppuru;* *korban*, gift or offering, is the Assyrian *kurbannu*. The names for animal sacrifice, *zibu*, for meal offering, *manitu*, and for freewill offering, *nidbu*, all are found in their Hebrew forms in the Old Testament. As in the Hebrew legislation, a distinction is made between the offerings of the rich and the poor, and the sacrificial animal was to be without blemish. The Babylonian priest retained certain parts for himself, which was also the custom among the Hebrews (Deut. 18. 3), though the parts retained are not the same in the two cases. A ritual tablet shows that Babylonians sprinkled the blood of the lamb that was killed at the gate of the palace on the lintels, on the figures flanking the entrances, and on the door-posts to the right and the left, which has its parallel in the Hebrew passover ceremony.

These illustrations, which by no means exhaust the list, reveal close similarities between the Hebrew ceremonial and that of the inhabitants of the Euphrates-Tigris valley, and the more we know of the Babylonian ritual, the more extensive and striking these resemblances become. They both start from the same principles and agree in many of their details. Between them, however, lies that deep gulf which separates the religion of

Israel from that of Babylonia as a whole. The one is monotheistic, the other polytheistic. Upon the basis of this fundamental difference the religious leaders of Israel gave to the similar forms adopted from other nations a new and deeper meaning and significance.

Like the Hebrew religion, the religion of Babylonia has its guardian angels.[23] The Babylonian rulers stood in need of hosts of messengers to bear their behests into all quarters of their dominions. In a similar manner, it was thought, the gods needed their heavenly hosts to carry out their commissions. These angels are represented under various forms, but all of them are equipped with wings, so as to be able to carry upon the winds of heaven the commands of the gods to the children of men. Sometimes they are represented with eagles' heads, perhaps to indicate that they possess the keenness of vision and the rapidity of flight of an eagle; sometimes they have human countenances to denote their human intelligence. Frequently they appear as hybrid figures, with the body of a lion or bull, the wings of an eagle, and the head of a man, symbolizing strength, swiftness, and intelligence.

The duties of these angels are manifold. Those placed at the entrances of palaces or temples are to guard those entrances. The peculiar relations of angels to men are suggested, for example, by

a letter of a Babylonian officer to the queen
mother. He writes: "Mother of the king, my lady,
be comforted. Bel's and Nabu's angel of mercy
attends on the king of the land, my lord." A
letter addressed to Esarhaddon contains these
words: "May the great gods send a guardian of
salvation and life to stand by the king my lord."
And Nabopolassar, the founder of the Chaldean
empire, and father of Nebuchadrezzar, writes:
"To lordship over land and people, Marduk called
me. He sent a cherub of mercy to attend on me,
and everything I undertook he aided."

Alongside of these guardian angels there appear
evil spirits and demons. "These demons were
everywhere: they lurked in every corner, watching
for their prey. The city streets knew their
malevolent presence, the rivers, the seas, the tops
of the mountains. They appeared sometimes as
serpents gliding noiselessly upon their victims; as
birds, horrid of mien, flying resistlessly to destroy
or afflict; as beings in human form, grotesque,
malformed, awe-inspiring through their hideous-
ness. To these demons all sorts of misfortunes
were ascribed: toothache, headache, broken bones,
raging fever, outbursts of anger, of jealousy. Did
a man lie wasting of disease and torn of pain, a
demon was thought to be within him, the disease
being but a manifestation of his malevolence.
There could be no return of the precious boon of

good health until the demon was exorcised, and it was to the exorcising of demons that so large, so disproportionate a part of the religious literature of Babylon and Nineveh was devoted."(24)   Sometimes demons are referred to in a manner which shows that the conception in Job 1. 6ff., Zech. 3. 1ff., of the Adversary, or the Satan, is closely related to the Babylonian conception of a demon as accuser, persecutor, or oppressor.

The vision of the Old Testament is largely confined to this world.   There is little hope for a man after he passes away from this earth.   Indeed, there are some passages which would seem to imply the thought that with death existence came entirely to an end.   Compare, for example, Psa. 39. 13:

> Oh, spare me, that I may recover strength
> Before I go hence, and be no more;

or Job 14. 7–12:

> For there is hope of a tree,
> If it be cut down, that it will sprout again,
> And that the tender branch thereof will not cease.
> Though the root thereof wax old in the earth,
> And the stock thereof die in the ground;
> Yet through the scent of water it will bud,
> And put forth boughs like a plant.
> But man dieth, and is laid low;
> Yea, man giveth up the ghost, and where is he?
> As the waters fail from the sea,
> And the river wasteth and drieth up;
> So man lieth down and riseth not:
> Till the heavens be no more, they shall not awake,
> Nor be roused out of their sleep.

These are expressions of deepest despondency and despair over a life soon ended, never to be lived again here upon earth.

However, by far the greatest number of Old Testament passages dealing with the subject express a belief in a continuous existence after death in Sheol. Sheol is the place of departed personalities; the generations of one's forefathers are there: he who dies is gathered unto his fathers; the tribal divisions of one's race are there: the dead is gathered unto his people; and if his descendants have died before him, they are there, and he goes down to them, as Jacob to his son (Gen. 37. 35: "For I will go down to Sheol to my son mourning"), and David to his child (2 Sam. 12. 23: "I shall go to him, and he shall not return to me").

There are only a few passages which go beyond this, expressing a hope of immortality or a resurrection.   There is, for example, the hope expressed in Psa. 16. 8–11:

> I have set Jehovah always before me:
> Because he is at my right hand, I shall not be moved.
> Therefore my heart is glad, and my glory rejoiceth:
> My flesh also shall dwell in safety.
> For thou will not leave my soul to Sheol;
> Neither wilt thou suffer thy holy one to see corruption.
> Thou wilt show me the path of life:
> In thy presence is fullness of joy;
> In thy right hand there are pleasures for evermore.

The hope expressed here is not a hope of a resurrection, but, rather, a hope that the psalmist will be delivered from death and live in fellowship with God forevermore. There are other passages which recognize the impossibility of escaping death, but express a hope that there will be a resurrection from death. The most definite Old Testament teaching of a resurrection is in Dan. 12. 2, "And many of them that sleep in the dust of the earth shall awake, some to everlasting life, and some to shame and everlasting contempt."

These lofty hopes are peculiar to Israel. But Israel's conception of Sheol shows very striking resemblances with the Babylonian conception. The descriptions found in Job, in the Psalms, in Isaiah, in Ezekiel and elsewhere, are hardly to be distinguished from those found in Babylonian literature. The opening lines of Ishtar's descent into Sheol read:

To the land from which there is no return, the home of
    darkness,
Ishtar, the daughter of Sin, turned her mind,
Yea, the daughter of Sin set her mind to go;
To the house of gloom, the dwelling of Irkalla,
To the house from which those who enter depart not,
The road from whose path there is no return;
To the house where they who enter are deprived of light;
A place where dust is their nourishment, clay their food;
The light they behold not, in thick darkness they dwell;
They are clad like bats in a garb of wings;
On door and bolt the dust is laid.

Compare with this Job 10. 21, 22:

Before I go, whence I shall not return,
    To the land of darkness, yea deepest darkness,

The land dark as midnight,
Of deepest darkness without any order,
And where the light is as midnight;

or Job 7. 9, 10:

He that goeth down to Sheol shall come up no more,
He shall return no more to his house,
Neither shall his place know him any more.

Other similarities may be noted: the Hebrew Sheol, like the Babylonian, was deep down in the earth; it is pictured as a cavern; silence reigns supreme, etc. There is but one explanation for these similarities: When the ancestors of the Hebrews left their homes in the Euphrates valley they carried with them the traditions, beliefs, and customs current in that district. Under new surroundings, and especially under the influence of their higher religion, new features were added and old conceptions were transformed. But these changes were not able to obscure entirely the character impressed upon the older beliefs by contact with Babylon.

Striking similarities are found also between the legal systems of Babylonia and Israel. In the light of recent discoveries the study of ancient law begins to-day, not with the legal systems of Rome, or of Greece, or of Israel, but with the laws of early Babylonia. Of the beginning of the Babylonian legal system we know nothing except a few popular traditions, which trace it back to some deity. It is clear, however, that long cen-

turies before the time of Moses or Minos or Romulus
the people living in the lower Euphrates-Tigris
valley developed legal codes of a high and complex
order. In the legal phrase books of the later
scribes there have been preserved seven so-called
Sumerian family laws, written in the language of
the people occupying the southern part of the
Euphrates-Tigris valley before it came under the
sway of the Semites. These laws, in theme and
literary form resembling later Babylonian and
early Hebrew laws, were probably in existence
in the fourth millennium B. C.; some of them may
go even farther back.

By far the most important Babylonian legal code
now known is the so-called Code of Hammurabi.([25])
Hammurabi was known to Assyriologists long before the finding of his legal code. He reigned in
Babylon about B. C. 2000, was the sixth king of the
first Babylonian dynasty, and the first permanently
to unite the numerous small city states under one
ruler. He may, therefore, be called the founder
of the Babylonian empire. From his numerous
letters and inscriptions, as also from other documents coming from the same period, he was
known as a great conqueror and statesman,
interested in the highest welfare of his people,
and persistently laboring for the improvement of
their conditions. The Bible student has a special
interest in Hammurabi, however, because in all

probability he is no other than the Amraphel of
Gen. 14. 1.

The monument on which the code is engraved
was found during the winter 1901–1902 by a
French excavator in the acropolis of Susa, the
scene of the book of Esther. It is a block of
black diorite, about eight feet in height. When
found it was in three pieces, which, however, were
easily joined. On the obverse is a bas relief
representing the king as receiving the ruler's staff
and ring from the sun-god Shamash, "the judge
of heaven and earth." Then follow on the obverse
sixteen columns of writing, containing 1,114 lines.
There were five more columns on this side, but
they were erased and the stone repolished, probably by the Elamite conqueror who carried the
monument to Susa. On the reverse are eighteen
columns with more than 2,500 lines of inscription.
The English Assyriologist, C. H. W. Johns, esti-
mates that originally the inscription contained
forty-nine columns, 4,000 lines, and about 8,000
words. About 800 lines are taken up by the
prologue and epilogue, setting forth the king's
titles, his glory, the extent of his rule, his care
for his subjects, and devotion to his gods. The
inscription opens with a statement of his call by
the gods to be the ruler of Babylon: "When the
lofty Anu, king of the Anunaki, and Bel, lord of
heaven and earth, he who determines the destiny

of the land, committed the rule of all mankind to Marduk, the chief son of Ea; when they made him great among the Igigi; when they pronounced the lofty name of Babylon, when they made it famous among the quarters of the world, and in its midst established an everlasting kingdom, whose foundations were firm as heaven and earth —at that time, Anu and Bel called me, Hammurabi, the exalted prince, the worshiper of the gods, to cause justice to prevail in the land, to destroy the wicked and the evil, to prevent the strong from oppressing the weak, to go forth like the sun over the blackhead race, to enlighten the land and to further the welfare of the people."

According to the closing statement of the prologue he faithfully executed this commission: "When Marduk sent me to rule the people and to bring help to the country, I established law and justice in the land and promoted the welfare of the people" (V. 14–21). To better care for the welfare of the people he set up the code of laws. In column XLI, a part of the epilogue, he says: "Let any oppressed man, who has a cause, come before my image as king of righteousness! Let him read the inscription on my monument! Let him give heed to my weighty words! And may my monument enlighten him as to his cause and may he understand his case! May he set his heart at ease!" (1–19.) He recognizes the value of his law code and advises his successors on the throne to make good use of it: "In the days that are yet to come, for all future time, may the king who is in the land observe the words of righteousness which I have written upon my monument! May he not alter the judgments of the land which I have pronounced, or the decisions of the country which I have rendered! May he not efface my statues! If that man have wisdom, if he wish to give his land good government, let him give attention to the words which I have written upon my monument! And may this monument enlighten him as to procedure and administration, the judgments which I have pronounced, and the judgments which I have rendered for the land! And let him rightly rule his blackhead people; let him pronounce judgments for them and render for them decisions! Let him root out the wicked and evildoer from the land! Let him promote the welfare of his people!"   (59–94.)

The epilogue closes with a blessing upon the king who will observe the laws, and curses upon him who will disregard or alter them (XLII–XLIV). The pronouncement of blessings is very brief; the curses are reiterated in various forms, and numerous gods and goddesses are appealed to by name to destroy the evildoer and his reign. The section begins (XLII, 2–49): "If that man pay attention to my words which I have written upon my monument, do not efface my judgments, do not overrule my words, and do not alter my statues, then will Shamash prolong that man's reign, as he has mine, who am king of righteousness, that he may rule his people in righteousness." It continues: "If that man do not pay attention to my words which I have written upon my monument; if he forget my curses and do not fear the curse of god; if he abolish the judgments which I have formulated, overrule my words, alter my statues, efface my name written thereon and write his own name; on account of these curses commission another to do so—as for that man, be he king or lord, or priestking or commoner, whoever he may be, may the great god, the father of the gods, who has ordained my reign, take from him the glory of his sovereignty, may he break his scepter and curse his fate!"

Between the prologue and the epilogue is the law code proper. Originally there appear to have been 282 separate enactments (this is the estimate of the French Assyriologist, Father Scheil, who first edited the code, and is commonly accepted as correct); of these 66–99 are now missing as a result of the erasure to which reference has been made. The code covers a variety of topics. Laws dealing with the same subject are ordinarily grouped together; sometimes the principle of arrangement is the class or profession concerned.

A brief outline will give at least a general notion
of its contents: 1, 2, False accusation of a crime;
3, 4, False witness and bribery; 5, Alteration of
judgment by a judge; 6–8, Theft; 9–13, Concealing
of stolen property; 14, Kidnapping; 15–20, Assist-
ing in the escape of slaves; 21–25, Burglary and
brigandage; 26–41, Rights and duties of officers,
constables, and taxgatherers; 42–52, Renting of
fields for cultivation; 53–56, Care of dykes and
canals; 57, 58, Shepherds allowing their sheep to
pasture on the fields of another; 59, Unlawful
cutting down of trees; 60–65, Duties of gardeners;
66–99, (lost); 100–107, Relation of merchants to
their agents; 108–111, Regulations concerning
wine-sellers, always women.   It may be interesting
to note that with them the law was very severe.
Of the three crimes condemned—minor crimes at
that—one is to be punished by throwing the wine-
seller into the water, the second by putting her
to death, the third by burning her.   112, Loss of
goods intrusted for transportation; 113–119, Securing settlement for debts; 120–126, Liability for
deposits; 127, Slander; 128, Marriage contract;
129–132, Adultery, rape, and suspected unchastity;
133–143, Separation and divorce; 144–149, Concubines; 150–152, Marriage dowry; 153, Murder of
husband for the sake of another; 154–158, Illegitimate sexual intercourse; 159–161, Breach of
promise; 162–164, Disposition of dowry after the

death of the wife; 165–177, Inheritance of sons in polygamous relations; 178–182, Inheritance of priestesses; 183, 184, Inheritance of daughters of concubines; 185–194, Treatment of adopted children; 195–214, Offenses against limb and life; 215–225, Operations by doctors and veterinary surgeons. For example, "If a physician cause a man a severe wound with a bronze lancet and cause the man's death, or, in opening an abscess of a man with a bronze lancet, destroy the man's eye, they shall cut off his fingers" (218). 226, 227, Unlawful branding of slaves; 228–233, Liability of negligent builders. For example, "If a builder build a house for a man, and do not make its construction firm, and the house which he has built collapse and cause the death of the owner of the house, that builder shall be put to death" (229). 234–252, Hired animals—the injuries they cause or suffer; 253–277, Rights and duties of workmen; 278–282, Selling and treatment of slaves.

In addition to this very complete code there is a vast amount of information from both early and late periods concerning legal practices, to be gathered from the thousands of tablets recording business and legal transactions of various sorts: Marriage and dowry contracts, partnership agreements, records of debts and promissory notes, leases of land, houses, or slaves; records of sales of all kinds of property, mortgages, documents granting the power of attorney; concerning adoption, divorce, bankruptcy, inheritance—in short, almost every imaginable kind of contract.

Over against this complex legal system of Babylonia we may place the legal literature of the Hebrews.([26]) Anyone who approaches the study of Hebrew laws is met by two difficulties. In the first place, the legal portions do not form separate books, but are embodied in writings belonging to other kinds of literature; in the second place, there is a lack of system in the arrangement of the laws. The abrupt transitions from one subject to another are almost as marked as they are in the book of Proverbs. "Civil and ceremonial, criminal and humane, secular and religious, ancient and late laws and precedents are all mingled together, with little trace of systematic arrangement."

The legal literature is found mainly in the books of Exodus, Leviticus, Numbers, and Deuteronomy; outside the Pentateuch the most important piece of legislation is Ezek. 40–48. This legal material may be separated from its surroundings and arranged by itself. Indeed, this has been done, and modern scholars are quite generally agreed that the Pentateuch contains several distinct legal codes belonging to different periods in the history of Israel and reflecting different stages of political, social, and religious development: (1) The Decalogue; (2) the Book of the Covenant; (3) the

Deuteronomic Code; (4) the Code of Holiness; (5) the Priestly Code. Of these five codes the last two are almost entirely religious and ceremonial, and as the similarities between the Babylonian and Hebrew ceremonial have already been pointed out, they need not be considered in this connection. The other three contain much legislation concerning social, civil, and criminal relations, just like the Babylonian legal provisions, and therefore may be considered somewhat more in detail. In connection with the Deuteronomic Code, however, it may be noted that three fourths of the laws in the earlier codes are reproduced in some form in Deuteronomy; so that for purposes of comparison, the Deuteronomic Code does not furnish many new elements. It is seen, therefore, that for a comparative study, the Code of Hammurabi on the one hand, and the Decalogue and the Book of the Covenant on the other, furnish the most important material; and since the Code of Hammurabi contains no religious and ceremonial provisions, the material of that nature in the Hebrew codes may be omitted in this connection.

That there exist similarities between the legislations of the two nations even a superficial reading will show. One is immediately struck, for example, by the similarity in the application of the *lex talionis:* Ham. 196, "If a man destroy the eye of another man, they shall destroy his eye"; 197, "If one

break a man's bone, they shall break his bone";
200, "If a man knock out the tooth of a man of
his own rank, they shall knock out his tooth."
With this compare Exod. 21. 23-25, "Thou shalt
give life for life, eye for eye, tooth for tooth,
burning for burning, wound for wound, stripe
for stripe"; or Deut. 19. 21, "Thine eyes shall
not pity; life shall go for life, eye for eye, tooth
for tooth, hand for hand, foot for foot." Compare
also Lev. 24. 19, 20, "If a man cause a blemish
in his neighbor; as he hath done, so shall it be
done to him: breach for breach; eye for eye,
tooth for tooth; as he hath caused a blemish in
a man, so shall it be rendered to him." This
principle is applied very extensively in both codes
in providing restitution for damage done.

The use of "the oath of innocence" is also
enjoined in both codes: Ham. 249, "If a man hire
an ox and a god strike it and it die, the man
who hired the ox shall swear before god and shall
go free." With this may be compared Exod. 22.
10, 11, "If a man deliver unto his neighbor an
ass, or an ox, or a sheep, or any beast to keep,
and it die, or be hurt, or driven away, no man
seeing it, the oath of Jehovah shall be between
them both, whether he hath not put his hand
unto his neighbor's goods, and the owner thereof
shall accept it, and he shall not make restitution."
The illustrations might be multiplied manifold.

Jeremias points out twenty-four similarities between the Code of Hammurabi and the Book of the Covenant alone; ([27]) which number is greatly increased if the comparison is extended so as to include the entire Pentateuch.

The spirit permeating the two systems is one of humaneness and kindness. Hammurabi describes himself as a shepherd chosen by the gods to care for his people, to lead them into safe pastures and to make them dwell in peace and security. He compiled the code, "that the great should not oppress the weak; to counsel the widow and orphan, to render judgment and to decide the decisions of the land, and to succor the injured." This is the same spirit that permeates the Pentateuchal legislation.

The picture at the head of the code, representing Hammurabi standing before the sun-god Shamash, "the supreme judge of heaven and earth," is very suggestive, for it reminds one of the narrative in Exodus which represents Moses as receiving the Hebrew laws directly from Jehovah.

Certainly, there are also differences between the two systems; and this is only what we should expect, since the civilization of Babylon was far in advance of and much more complex than that of the Israelites, even during the period of the latter's highest development. Besides, the lower religious conceptions would inevitably influence the legislation.

Attention may be called also to some similarities between the Decalogue and certain requirements in Babylonia, the existence of which is implied in an incantation (²⁸) in which these questions are asked: Has he broken into the house of his neighbor? Has he approached the wife of his neighbor? Has he spilled the blood of his neighbor? Has he grasped the garment of his neighbor? These questions would seem to imply the existence of laws like these: Thou shalt not break into the house of thy neighbor; Thou shalt not approach the wife of thy neighbor; Thou shalt not spill the blood of thy neighbor; Thou shalt not grasp the garment of thy neighbor.

In view of all these similarities, the question naturally arises whether the Babylonian legal system exerted any influence upon the lawmakers of the Hebrews, for the resemblances are too close to be explained entirely on the basis of coincidence. Those who admit some relation between the two legislations are not in agreement as to the nature of the connection. Some hold that there is direct dependence; that the author or authors of the laws of the Pentateuch was or were acquainted with the laws of Hammurabi, and made these laws the basis of the Hebrew legislative system. The possibility of such dependence cannot be denied. Surely, an acquaintance with the Code of Hammurabi in the Arabian

desert or in Palestine at the time of the exodus
or later cannot appear strange in view of the
evidence of the Tel-el-Amarna tablets, showing
that some time before the exodus intercourse
between Babylon and the West was frequent; that
religious, political, and literary influence was widespread, and that the language of Babylon was
the *lingua franca* throughout Canaan. On the
other hand, there are those who believe that the
parallels and analogies between the two codes are
due to the common Semitic origin of the two
systems. The Babylonians and the Hebrews were
Semites, originally dwelling in a common home.
When they left this home they carried with them
their common traditions, laws, customs, and practices. In their new homes they developed them
and impressed upon them their own individuality.
The result among the Hebrews, determined in a
large measure by their peculiar religion, is seen
in the legislation of the Pentateuch, while the
outcome in Babylon is best represented by the
Code of Hammurabi.

Which of these two explanations is correct it
may be impossible to say with absolute certainty.
To me it seems that both contain elements of
truth. Sometimes the one, sometimes the other
may be correct, while in other cases the similarities may be due to coincidence. In any case,
the value of the Pentateuchal legislation remains

unaffected, for it depends, not upon its origin or process of growth, but, rather, upon its inherent spirit and character.

Attention may further be called to the existence in Babylonia of stories showing almost startling resemblances to the accounts of the creation of the world, of the origin of man and of sin, of a Deluge, and other narratives contained in the first eleven chapters of the book of Genesis. Several distinct creation stories, originating in different religious centers, have been handed down. The most remarkable of these, called *Enuma elish* (when above), from its opening words, has been deciphered from tablets found in the library of Ashurbanipal in the ruins of Nineveh. These tablets represent a copy made in the seventh century B. C. The time of the composition, or compilation of the story, is not known. However, pictorial representations of some of the scenes in the epic, and allusions in other literary productions whose dates can be fixed, make it certain that the story, or at least the most important component elements of the story, existed before B. C. 2000. In its present form it belongs to a period later than the elevation of Babylon to be the national center, which took place under Hammurabi, about B. C. 2000, for the chief place is assigned to Marduk, the god of Babylon.([29])

Echoes of this story are found in several Old

Testament passages, especially in the poetic and prophetic writings. In these Jehovah is represented as having contended with a great primeval monster, called in some passages Rahab, in others Leviathan, or Dragon. This being seems to symbolize chaos, or to personify the primeval ocean, which existed when the process of creation began. In the conflict between Jehovah and this monster the hostile creature and its helpers were overthrown, after which the heavens and the earth were created. A few of these passages may be quoted:

> O Jehovah God of hosts,
> Who is a mighty one, like unto thee, O Jehovah?
> And thy faithfulness is round about thee.
> Thou rulest the pride of the sea:
> When the waves thereof arise, thou stillest them.
> *Thou hast broken Rahab in pieces, as one that is slain;*
> *Thou hast scattered thine enemies with the arm of thy strength.*
> The heavens are thine, the earth also is thine:
> The world and the fullness thereof, thou hast founded them,
> The north and the south, thou hast created them (Psa. 89. 8–12).

Rahab is a reflection of the Babylonian Tiamat; Jehovah takes the place of the Babylonian god, Marduk, the conqueror of Tiamat; the *enemies* are the *helpers* of Tiamat mentioned in the Babylonian poem. The order of events is the same in the two accounts: first the conflict, then creation.

He stirreth up the sea with his power,
And by his understanding *he smiteth through Rahab.*

By his Spirit the heavens are garnished;
His hand hath pierced the swift serpent (Job 26. 12, 13).

God will not withdraw his anger;
The helpers of Rahab do stoop under him (Job 9. 13).

Yet God is my King of old,
Working salvation in the midst of the earth.
Thou didst divide the sea by thy strength:
Thou brakest the heads of the sea-monsters in the waters.
Thou brakest the heads of leviathan in pieces;
Thou gavest him to be food to the people inhabiting the
    wilderness.
Thou didst cleave fountain and flood:
Thou driedst up mighty rivers.
The day is thine, the night also is thine:
Thou hast prepared the light and the sun.
Thou hast set all the borders of the earth:
Thou hast made summer and winter (Psa. 74. 12–17).

The similarities between the Babylonian story called *Enuma elish* and the narrative of creation in Gen. 1 are especially pronounced: (1) Both accounts recognize a time when all was chaos. In the Babylonian conception this chaos is personified in Tiamat; in Gen. 1. 2 occurs the word *tehom,* translated "deep," which is the same as Tiamat, changed but slightly in passing from one language to the other. (2) In Genesis light dispels darkness and order follows; in the Babylonian account, Marduk, the god of light, overcomes the demon of chaos and darkness. (3) The second act of creation is the making of the firmament, which "divided the waters which were under the firmament from the waters which were above the firmament" (Gen. 1. 6–8); in the Babylonian poem the body of Tiamat is divided and one half becomes the firmament to keep the heavenly waters in place. (4) The third and fourth acts of creation in the Hebrew story are the creation of earth and the beginning of vegetation (Gen. 1. 9–13); the corresponding Babylonian story has been lost, but it seems quite probable that these acts were described in the same order on the fifth tablet. Berosus, in his summary of the Babylonian account, says that Bel formed the earth out of one half of Omorka's body—Omorka is probably a corruption of *Ummu-Khubur*, a title of Tiamat—and as in every instance where the narrative of Berosus has been tested it has proved to be correct, we may assume that in this also he gives a correct reproduction of the Babylonian tradition. Moreover, at the beginning of the seventh tablet Marduk is hailed as "bestower of fruitfulness," "founder of agriculture," "creator of grain and plants," he "who caused the green herb to spring up." (5) The fifth act of creation is the making of the heavenly bodies (Gen. 1. 14–19). With this the Babylonian parallel shows close similarities, for it states that Marduk

> Made the stations for the great gods,
> The stars, their images, as the constellations he fixed,
> He ordained the year, marked off its divisions.[30]

(6) The sixth and seventh acts of creation were the creation of fishes and birds and of land animals (Gen. 1. 20–25); the Babylonian parallels in *Enuma elish* are wanting at present; but Berosus hints that they were created at the same time as man, so that it is probable that the account of these acts of creation appeared somewhere in the lost portions of the fifth or sixth tablet. From allusions in other writings we learn that Marduk was looked upon as the creator of the animals and other living creatures of the field. (7) The eighth act of creation, that of man (Gen. 1. 26–31), finds its parallel upon the sixth tablet:

When Marduk heard the word of the gods
His heart moved him and he devised a cunning plan.
He opened his mouth and unto Ea he spoke,
That which he had conceived in his heart he made known
    unto him.
"My blood will I take and bone will I fashion,
I shall make man that man may   .   .   .
I shall create man, who shall inhabit the earth,
That the service of the gods may be established and that
    their shrines may be built."[31]

In order to estimate rightly the relations between the Babylonian and Hebrew accounts the differences between the two must also be noted. To begin with, the order of the separate acts of creation is not quite the same. For example, in the Babylonian account, the creation of the heavenly bodies follows immediately upon the making of the firmament, while in the Hebrew story it follows the making of the earth and the springing up of vegetation. Certainly, this difference is of no special significance, and the change may easily be explained as due to the desire of the Hebrew writer to crowd the creative acts into the six working days of the week. The real difference is more fundamental and appears especially in the conception of the nature and character of Deity. The Babylonian story opens with these words:

> When above the heaven was not named
> And beneath the earth bore no name,
> And the primeval Apsu, who begat them,
> And Mummu-Tiamat, the mother of them all—
> Their waters were mingled together,
> And no reed was formed, no marsh seen,
> *When no one of the gods had been called into being,*
> [And] none bore a name, and no destinies [were fixed].
> *Then were created the gods in the midst of* [*heaven*].

Compare with this the simple, yet majestic, conception, "In the beginning God created the heavens and the earth." In one case many gods, in the other one God almighty; in one case the gods are a part of the process of creation, in the other the uncreated God is in the beginning. Genesis presents God as almighty, but also as kind, beneficent, loving; Marduk, the Babylonian creator, is represented as a great hero, but exceedingly selfish. He undertakes the mighty task of

overcoming Tiamat only after making arrange-
ments for a suitable reward. The description of
the heavenly banquet scene, to which reference
has been made earlier in the chapter, implies a
conception of the character of the gods which is
separated by an impassable gulf from the Old
Testament ideal.

No one can read with an unbiased mind the
two accounts without realizing the great differences between the mythological, polytheistic account of the Babylonians and the simple, solemn,
sublime, monotheistic picture in Genesis. The
soberness, the dignity, the simplicity of the
Hebrew account lift it far above its Babylonian
counterpart. From it the crude nature myths
have all been stripped away. No drunken gods
hold revels in its solemn lines. Above and behind
and in all is one righteous and beneficent God.
In this sublime ethical monotheism the Hebrew
story rises infinitely above the story that originated
in the Euphrates-Tigris valley.

Another Babylonian tradition, the close relation
of which to the biblical account has long been
recognized, is the story of the Deluge. In its
cuneiform text it was first discovered on fragments
of tablets brought from the library of Ashurbanipal.
But that the Babylonians possessed a story of
the Flood was known before from an outline
preserved by Berosus. The tradition brought to

light by archæology forms an episode in an epic
which narrates the exploits of Gilgamesh and
occupies the eleventh of the twelve parts into
which the epic is divided. Gilgamesh sprang
from a city, Shurippak, which afterward completely disappeared. He became king of Erech,
where he ruled as a tyrant until the gods created
Ea-bani to destroy him. The two, however,
became bosom friends. Together they delivered
Erech from the Elamite oppressor, Khumbaba.
Ishtar, the goddess of love, then offered her hand
to Gilgamesh in marriage, which he spurned with
scorn. Out of revenge, she sent a scorpion,
whose sting proved fatal to Ea-bani. Gilgamesh
himself she smote with an incurable disease. To
find relief, the latter set out for the dwelling
place of his great-grandfather, Ut-napishtim, far
away on the isles of the blessed. When he finally
reaches him the latter tells him all about the
great Flood from which he escaped to enjoy
eternal life.([32])

The most striking resemblances between the
Babylonian and Hebrew stories of the Flood may
now be noted: (1) Compare the instruction given
by God to Noah (Gen. 6. 13–22) with the words
addressed by the god Ea to Ut-napishtim:

> O man of Shurippak, son of Ubaratutu,
> Pull down thy house, build a ship,
> Leave thy possessions, take thought for thy life,

> Thy property abandon, save thy life,
> Bring living seed of every kind into the ship.
> The ship that thou shalt build,
> So shall be the measure of its dimensions,
> Thus shall correspond its breadth and height,
> Into the ocean let it fare.[33]

(2) In both accounts the destruction is due to sin. This is definitely stated in Gen. 6. 5–7. For the Babylonian story it is implied in the rebuke given to Bel by Ea:

> On the sinner lay his sin,
> On the transgressor lay his transgression.
> Forbear, let not all be destroyed.[34]

(3) In both accounts, only a seed of life sufficient to replenish the earth is saved. Compare Gen. 6. 19, 20 with the command, "Bring living seed of every kind into the ship," or with the statement:

I brought into the ship my family and household;
The cattle of the field, the beasts of the field, craftsmen, all
    of them I brought in.[35]

(4) Both stories tell of a great storm and deluge of water. Gen. 7. 11 reads, "The fountains of the great deep were broken up, and the windows of heaven were opened. And the rain was upon the earth forty days and forty nights." Compare with this:

> The dawning of that day I feared,
> I feared to behold that day.
> I entered the ship and closed the door. . . .
> When the first flush of dawn appeared
> There came up from the horizon a black cloud.

Adad thundered within it,
While Nabu and Marduk went before.
They go as messengers over mountain and valley.
Nergal bore away the anchor.
Ninib advances, the storm he makes to descend.
The Anunaki lifted up their torches,
With their brightness they light up the land.
Adad's storm reached unto heaven,
All light was turned into darkness,
It [flooded] the land like . . .
. . . . the storm
Raged high, [the water climbed over] the mountains,
Like a besom of destruction they brought it upon men.(36)

(5) In both instances the structure rests upon a
mountain in the north.   Gen. 8. 4 reads, "And
the ark rested . . . upon the mountains of Ararat,"
that is, Armenia.   The Babylonian story reads:

To the land of Nisir the ship made its way,
The mount of Nisir held it fast that it moved not.(37)

Mount Nisir is east of the upper Tigris.   (6) In
both cases birds are sent out to ascertain the condition of the land.   Compare Gen. 8. 6–12 with
these lines:

When the seventh day approached
I sent forth a dove and let her go.
The dove flew to and fro,
But there was no resting place and she returned.
I sent forth a swallow and let her go;
The swallow flew to and fro,
But there was no resting place, and she returned.
I sent forth a raven and let her go;
The raven flew away, she saw the abatement of the waters,

She drew near, she waded (?), she croaked, and came not
   back.
Then I sent everything forth to the four quarters of
   heaven.([38])

(7) Sacrifice is offered by Noah and Ut-napishtim,
acceptable to the God of Noah and to the gods
of the Babylonian hero, in both cases resulting
in a promise not to repeat the Flood. Compare
Gen. 8. 20–22 with:

                  I offered sacrifice,
I made a libation upon the mountain's peak.
By sevens I set out the sacrificial vessels,
Beneath them I heaped up reed and cedar wood and myrtle.
The gods smelt the savor,
The gods smelt the sweet savor,
The gods gathered like flies over the sacrificer.([39])

Other similarities might be noted, such as the
use of bitumen, the arrangement of the ship in
stories, and, what seems more striking, the fact
that the hero of the Babylonian story is the
tenth antediluvian king, while Noah is the tenth
antediluvian patriarch.

As in the stories of creation, marked differences
may also be noted between the two representations
of the Flood; and these differences appear where
they are most significant, namely, in the spirit
and purity of conception permeating the entire
Hebrew account. For example, the book of
Genesis introduces the divine displeasure with sin,
the ethical element, as a fundamental note; then,

when the divine mercy is aroused, the Flood ceases; according to the Babylonian story, the Flood is caused by the capricious anger of Bel, the idea of punishment for sin cropping out only as an incident in the conversation between Ea and Bel at the end of the story. The Flood ceases because the other gods are terrified, and Ishtar intercedes for her own creation. Moreover, the whole Hebrew conception of the Divine differs from the Babylonian. In the Hebrew account we find ourselves in an atmosphere of ethical monotheism that is unknown apart from the chosen people. Disappeared have all the gods who war with one another, who rejoice in successful intrigues, who do not hesitate to tell untruths or instruct their favorites to do so; the gods unstable in all their ways, now seeking to destroy, now flattering their creatures; the gods who, terrified by the storm, "cower like dogs" at the edge of heaven, and who "gathered like flies" around the sacrifice of the saved hero. All these characteristic features of the Babylonian account are absent from the Bible. Surely, there is no connection between these deities and the one sublime and gracious God of Genesis.

Lack of space will not permit us to institute detailed comparisons between other narratives in the early chapters of Genesis and Babylonian literature. It may be sufficient to say that the resemblances are not confined to the stories of creation and of the Flood. True, no complete Babylonian story of paradise and of the fall is at present known; nevertheless, there are certain features in the biblical narrative which strongly point to Babylonia, and in the light of the known fact that elements in the two important narratives of creation and of the Flood are derived from Babylonia, it may be safe to infer that in this case also echoes of Babylonian beliefs supplied, at least in part, the framework of the Hebrew representation. The antediluvian patriarchs also seem to have their counterparts in Babylonian tradition, and the story of the Tower of Babel, though it does not seem to be of Babylonian origin, presupposes a knowledge of Babylonia, and it is not impossible that some Babylonian legend served as the basis of it.

In closing this discussion, attention may be called to a few general considerations that must be borne in mind in any attempt to answer the question whether the religious and ethical ideas of the Hebrews which show similarities with the ideas of other nations were borrowed bodily from these nations, or, after all, contain elements that were original with the Hebrews.

In the first place, it must be remembered that similarities between the customs or beliefs of two peoples do not necessarily imply the dependence of one upon the other; much less do they indicate which is the original. Where similarities are found at least four possibilities should be recognized: A may depend upon B; B may depend upon A; both A and B may have been derived from a common original; or A and B may have developed independently, the similarities being merely coincidence. Which interpretation is the right one in a given case does not lie on the surface; it is only by careful, patient, unbiased study that one may arrive at a proper understanding. Take as an illustration the Decalogue. The Buddhists have "ten prohibitory laws," sometimes called the "Buddhist Decalogue." The first five read, "Thou shalt not kill; Thou shalt not steal; Thou shalt not lie; Thou shalt not commit adultery; Thou shalt not get drunk." Three of these correspond exactly to three of the demands in the Jewish Decalogue. Does it necessarily follow that the Decalogue was borrowed from Buddha? The Egyptians also had a sacred law. The law itself has not yet come to light, but the Book of the Dead indicates its existence. In the one hundred and twenty-fifth chapter of this book we read the justifications offered by the dead: "I have not acted with deceit or done evil to men; I have not oppressed the poor; I have not judged unjustly," etc. These negations seem to imply the existence of a law, either oral or written, forbidding these things. From the negations, "I have not acted with deceit; I have not committed murder; I have not been unchaste," etc., one may infer that the Egyptians had precepts corresponding substantially to some of the requirements in the Decalogue. Does logic demand, therefore, the conclusion that the Decalogue owes its existence to the sacred law of the Egyptians? Among the Babylonians also we find evidence of the existence of, at least, some of the requirements of the Hebrew Decalogue: "Thou shalt not break into the house of thy neighbor; Thou shalt not approach the wife of thy neighbor; Thou shalt not spill the blood of thy neighbor; Thou shalt not grasp the garment of thy neighbor." Do these similarities prove beyond question the dependence of the one upon the other?

There are, then, marked resemblances between the Hebrew Decalogue, certain requirements among the Babylonians, among the Egyptians, and among the Buddhists. I know of no one who claims that the Decalogue was borrowed from Buddha; some, however, seem to think, that in part at least, it was dependent upon Babylon; others, that Moses is indebted for it to Egypt. True, in the minds of most scholars the dependence is not direct; there would be room, according to their theory, for the work of the Spirit in the selection of these fundamental, ethical conceptions from the great mass of requirements, the majority of which are far inferior to the Decalogue. Such dependence, even if it could be proved, would not rob the Decalogue of inspiration or permanent value; but it seems to me that the similarities do not warrant the claim of even such dependence. Is it not more likely that these similarities are due to the instinct implanted in man by the Creator, which recognizes the sanctity of life, of family relations, and of property rights? But this instinct does not account for the obvious differences between the Hebrew Decalogue as a whole and the legislations of other peoples. These must be traced to the special activity of a Spirit who produced among the Hebrews a collection of commandments such as natural instinct, if left to itself, could not have produced.

It is different, perhaps, when we consider the relation of the more comprehensive civil legislation of the Pentateuch to the Code of Hammurabi. There the resemblances are numerous and striking enough to justify the inference that there exists some relation of dependence, and yet by no means that the legislation of the Pentateuch is borrowed directly from the other, or even that there is a literary dependence. How extensive this dependence is only careful examination can show; but, however complete, it will not destroy the fact that the laws of Israel are permeated by a Divine

Spirit. The important question is not, Where do we find the natural basis upon which the system is built up by men under divine guidance? but, Does the spirit and character of the system indicate such guidance?

In the second place, in seeking the truth about this relationship assumption must not be confused with knowledge. Modern archæologists seem to be in peculiar danger of taking things for granted. It is not without reason that a prominent Old Testament scholar proposes to change the title of the third edition of a book entitled The Cuneiform Inscriptions and the Old Testament into The Cuneiform Scholar and the Old Testament. It is stated, for example, without qualification by Delitzsch that the name "Yahweh" has been discovered on inscriptions belonging to the period of Hammurabi. No hint is given that the reading is questioned by many Assyriologists. There is, at least, a possibility, no matter how small, of a different rendering, with, of course, a vastly different conclusion. But admitting, as I believe we must do, that the name does occur, the inference drawn from this occurrence by Delitzsch, and expressed in the following words, is an assumption and misleading, unless it is materially modified: "Yahweh, the abiding one, the permanent one, who, unlike man, is not to-morrow a thing of the past, but one that endures forever, that lives and labors for all eternity above the broad, resplendent, law-bound canopy of the stars—it was this Yahweh that constituted the primordial patrimony of those Canaanite tribes from which centuries afterward the twelve tribes of Israel sprang."[40] The fact is that you may search the Babylonian pantheon from one end to the other and you will not find one god who in nature and character can compare with the Jehovah of Israel, "merciful and gracious, slow to anger, and abundant in loving-kindness and truth."

Another instance of the same character is the story of the fall. One thing we know, namely, that a story of the fall of man, similar to that in Genesis, has not as yet been found among the fragments of Babylonian libraries. Certainly, such story may have existed, and probably did exist; it may even be, as has been asserted, that some connection exists between the scriptural story of the fall and the picture on an old Babylonian seal cylinder having in the center a tree with fruits hanging down, on each side a figure, and behind the figure at the left a mark which may represent a serpent. But the interpretation is by no means certain. The fact that an assertion is made by an expert favors the presumption, but does not prove, that the statement is true.

Some archæologists claim that the monotheism of Israel was derived from outside of Israel, either from Arabia([41]) or from Babylonia ([42]). Among the arguments in favor of this claim is the occurrence of proper names which are alleged to imply the existence of monotheism; for example, *Yasma-ilu*, which may be translated "God hears," implying the existence of but one God.   However, it might mean also "*a* god hears," or "god"— referring to one of many—"hears," the giver of the name singling out the one for special consideration.   And as there are clear indications of polytheism in southern Arabia, where the name is found, the name, in all probability, means the latter, thus implying polytheism.   The same may be said of the names found in Babylonia.   Whatever the primary meaning of *ilu*, these names do not in themselves prove the existence of monotheism.   They may be translated in perfect accord with logic and grammar as admitting the existence of more than one god.   Indeed, the historical facts demand such interpretation.   If we find, for example, "Sin-muballit" ("the moon-god brings to life") as the name of the father of Hammurabi, and "Shamshu-iluna" (in all probability, "the sun-god is our god") as that of his son, the facts surely indicate that the monotheism of the period was not very distinct.   The testimony of the Code of Hammurabi points in the same direction, as also the most spiritual utterances of religion in the Euphrates valley, the penitential psalms.

It is seen, then, that facts do not warrant the claim, made by some, that that upon which rests the significance of the Bible in the world's history, namely, monotheism, was taken over by the Hebrews from the Babylonians. Josh. 24. 2 remains uncontradicted: "Your fathers dwelt of old time beyond the River, even Terah, the father of Abraham, and the father of Nahor; and *they served other gods.*" It is only in Israel that we find a clearly developed monotheism. Assumption and facts are not quite the same.

Another important point, to which attention has already been called, is the marked difference which obtains between the literature of the Old Testament and that uncovered by archæology. True, there are points of contact; indeed, strange it would be if there were none; for, like the Babylonians, the Hebrews were Semites. Surely, it is not strange that nations of the same race, originally in the same home, should possess similar traditions, customs, beliefs, and practices. When they left their common home they carried with them their common traditions, customs, and beliefs; in their new homes they developed them and impressed upon them their own individualities. We are nowhere informed in the Old Testament, and it would seem contrary to reason to suppose, that at the time of Abraham, Moses, or at any other period, God emptied the Hebrew mind and con-

sciousness of all the things which had been the
possession of the Semitic race from the beginning.
Is it not more likely that the inspired teachers
and writers employed for their loftier purposes
the ancient traditions and beliefs familiar to their
contemporaries? In doing so they took that
which was, in some cases, common and unclean,
and, purifying it under the guidance of the Divine
Spirit, made it the medium by which to impart
the sublimest truths ever presented to man. Ob-
viously, the special religious value of the Old
Testament literature does not lie in what is common
to it and Babylon, but in the elements in which
they differ.

The points of contact must not blind the eye
to the points of contrast. These points of contrast are in the spirit and atmosphere pervading
the Hebrew Scriptures, which are quite distinct,
not simply from Babylonian, but from all other
literatures. These essential differences occur, as
we have seen, throughout the entire religious
and ethical literature. In many cases is agreement in form, but how far superior the spirit
and substance of the Hebrew! Think of the
different conceptions of the nature and character
of God, of God's relation to man, of the divine
government of the world, and many other truths
precious to Christians in all ages. There is, indeed,
in the Hebrew record "an intensity of spiritual con-

ception, a sublimity of spiritual tone, an insight into the unseen, a reliance upon an invisible yet all-controlling Power, that create the gap between the Hebrew and his brother Semite beyond the River."

How are we to account for these differences? Professor Sayce has suggested an answer in these words: "I can find only one explanation, unfashionable and antiquated though it be. In the language of a former generation, it marks the dividing line between revelation and unrevealed religion. It is like that something hard to define which separates man from the ape, even though on the physiological side the ape may be the ancestor of man."[43] Though the language of this statement may be unfortunate, especially where it implies that there is no revelation in the ancient religions outside of the Old Testament, it does call attention to the secret of the fundamental difference between the Old Testament sacred literature and that of the surrounding nations. There is in the former abundant evidence of the activity of a Spirit whose presence is less manifest in the sacred literatures of other ancient nations.

True, the monuments have not spoken their last word; but if we have the right to draw inferences from the known, we may safely affirm that though the monuments may swell into infinity, they will offer nothing to equal, much less to supersede, in substance and spirit, our

Old Testament. We may receive gratefully every ray of light, but the time has not yet come, nor ever will come, when we may lay aside the Old Testament and accept as a substitute the legends and myths of heathen lands to give to us the bread of life which the Saviour found in the pages of the Old Book. Let us welcome the light and knowledge God has bestowed upon us; let us rejoice in them with perfect assurance that they are for good and not for evil; let us learn to use them wisely and honestly, and let us still be ever alert listening for other words, uttered ages ago, but not yet audible to modern ears. "It is for us to catch these messages, and to understand them, that we may fit them into the great fabric of apprehended truth to the enrichment of ourselves, and to the glory of our common Lord."

NOTES ON CHAPTER V

(1) J. P. Peters, The Old Testament and the New Scholarship, p. 92.

(2) S. G. Smith, Religion in the Making, p. 20.

(3) Hugo Winckler, Himmels- und Weltenbild der Babylonier, p. 9.

(4) Professor Friedrich Delitzsch, of the University of Berlin, delivered three lectures on the relation of Babylonian religion to the religion of the Old Testament, under the title, "Babel und Bibel."

(5) A. H. Sayce, The Religions of Ancient Egypt and Babylonia, pp. 276, 277.

(6) A. Jeremias, The Old Testament in the Light of the Ancient East, I, p. 86.

(⁷) R. W. Rogers, The Religion of Babylonia and Assyria, p. 88. Practically all the cuneiform inscriptions quoted or referred to in this chapter are translated in R. W. Rogers, Cuneiform Parallels to the
Old Testament.

(⁸) Friedrich Delitzsch, Babel and Bible, Two Lectures,
published by Open Court Co., p. 65.

(⁹) A translation of the entire psalm is found in Sayce,
The Religions of Ancient Egypt and Babylonia, pp.
419–421; also in Rogers, Religion of Babylonia
and Assyria, pp. 182–184; R. F. Harper, Assyrian
and Babylonian Literature, pp. 436–439.

(¹⁰) Sayce, Religions of Ancient Egypt and Babylonia,
pp. 35, 93, 195. A translation of a hymn composed
by this king to his supreme god is found in J. H.
Breasted, A History of Egypt, pp. 371ff.

(¹¹) An excellent brief survey of the religious conceptions
of the pre-Mosaic period is given in the article on
"Religion of Israel," by E. Kautzsch, in James
Hastings, Dictionary of the Bible, Extra Vol.,
pp. 613ff.

(¹²) The Religion of Babylonia and Assyria, p. 95.

(¹³) Ibid., p. 97.

(¹⁴) The most recent and most satisfactory edition and
translation of the entire Babylonian story of creation is by L. W. King, The Seven Tablets of Creation. The two quotations given are Tablet I, lines
7–9, and Tablet III, lines 133–138.

(¹⁵) Additional portions of this hymn are found in R. W.
Rogers, Religion of Babylonia and Assyria, pp. 170ff.

(¹⁶) S. I. Curtiss, Primitive Semitic Religions To-day, p. 14.

(¹⁷) A. T. Clay, Light on the Old Testament from Babel,
p. 15; A. H. Sayce, Religions of Ancient Egypt and
Babylonia, pp. 476ff.; M. Jastrow, in American
Journal of Theology, 1898, pp. 315–352; A. Jeremias, The Old Testament in the Light of the Ancient East, I, pp. 198ff.

([18]) Babel and Bible, Two Lectures, p. 38.

([19]) Ibid., p. 101.

([20]) Paul Haupt, Babylonian Elements in the Levitical Ritual, Journal of Biblical Literature, 1900, p. 61.

([21]) The details of this question have been discussed very extensively. Admirable discussions of the entire subject are found in Sayce, Religions of Ancient Egypt and Babylonia, pp. 448–478; Jeremias, Old Testament in the Light of the Ancient East, II, pp. 112ff.

([22]) Religions of Ancient Egypt and Babylonia, p, 469.

([23]) Delitzsch, Babel and Bible, Two Lectures, pp. 53ff.

([24]) R. W. Rogers, Religion of Babylonia and Assyria, p. 145.

([25]) R. F. Harper, The Code of Hammurabi; art. on the same subject in Hastings, Dictionary of the Bible, Extra Vol., pp. 584ff.; W. W. Davies, The Codes of Hammurabi and Moses.

([26]) The best and most complete recent treatment of the legal literature of the Old Testament is found in C. F. Kent, Israel's Laws and Legal Precedents, which is Vol. IV in The Student's Old Testament.

([27]) Johannes Jeremias, Moses and Hammurabi, pp. 31ff.

([28]) R. W. Rogers, Religion of Babylonia and Assyria, p. 158.

([29]) L. W. King, The Seven Tablets of Creation, Two Vols.; a translation is also found in R. F. Harper, Assyrian and Babylonian Literature, pp. 282ff. R. W. Rogers, Religion of Babylonia and Assyria, pp. 107ff.

([30]) Tablet V, lines 1–3.

([31]) Lines 1–8.

([32]) An English translation of the entire epic is found in R. F. Harper, Assyrian and Babylonian Literature, pp. 324ff.; the Deluge story is given by R. W. Rogers, Religion of Babylonia and Assyria, pp 199ff.

([33]) Lines 23–31.

([34]) Lines 184–186.

([35]) Lines 27, 85, 86.

([36]) Lines 92–111.

([37]) Lines 141, 142.

([38]) Lines 146–156.

([39]) Lines 156–162.

([40]) Babel and Bible, Two Lectures, p. 62.

([41]) F. Hommel, The Ancient Hebrew Tradition, pp. 75ff.

([42]) F. Delitzsch, Babel and Bible, pp. 58ff.

([43]) Preface to Religions of Ancient Egypt and Babylonia.

CHAPTER VI

The Permanent Significance of the Old Testament

IN the opening paragraphs of Chapter I, attention is called to the unique place occupied by the Old Testament in the thought, life, and theology of the early Church. Throughout the Middle Ages, and in the eyes of the Protestant reformers, the two great divisions of the Bible, the Old and New Testaments, continued to command equal respect and attention. The legal principles of the Pentateuch have determined the legal systems of all civilized nations; the bold and fiery sermons of the prophets have been the chief inspiration on the fierce battles for righteousness in all ages; and the sublime religious lyrics of the Psalter have ushered millions into the very presence of God. Indeed, the Old Testament has exerted an incalculable influence on the development of religion and civilization.

However, it must be admitted that during the latter part of the nineteenth century a change of attitude toward the Old Testament seems to have taken place. True, from nearly the beginning of the Christian era again and again voices have

been heard denying to the Old Testament a place
in Christian thought and life, but not until comparatively recent times has this sentiment become
widespread. Says a writer in a book published
a few years ago: "The Bible was never more
studied nor less read than at the present day.
This paradox is true, at least, of the Old Testament. For two generations scores of patient
scholars have toiled on the text, scanning each
letter with microscopic care, and one result of
their labors has been that to the majority of
educated men and women of whatever belief, or
no belief, the Bible has become a closed, yea, a
sealed, book. It is not what it used to be; what
it has become they do not know, and in scorn
or sorrow or apathy they have laid it aside."(¹)
There may be some exaggeration in this statement,
but it cannot be doubted that there is considerable justification for the complaint. C. F. Kent
makes the admission that "with the exception of
a very few books, like the Psalter, the Old Testament, which was the arsenal of the old militant
theology, has been unconsciously, if not deliberately, shunned by the present generation."(²)
And the words of Professor Cheyne are almost
as applicable to-day as they were when they
were first written, more than twenty years ago:
"A theory is already propounded, both in private
and in a naïve simple way in sermons, that the

Old Testament is of no particular moment, all that we need being the New Testament, which has been defended by our valiant apologists and expounded by our admirable interpreters."(³)

If this represents in any sense the true state of affairs; if, on the other hand, the words of the apostle are true, that "every scripture inspired of God is also profitable for teaching, for reproof, for correction, for instruction which is in right-eousness, that the man of God may be complete, furnished completely unto every good work"; and if these words are applicable to the Old Testament, as the writer intended them to be—if, I say, these things are true, then Christians appear to be in great peril of losing sight of one of the important means of grace, on which were nourished Jesus and his disciples, and millions in former generations, and for the restoration of which the reformers risked their very lives.

The change of attitude toward the Old Testa-ment may be traced to a variety of causes, all of which affect very vitally modern religious thought and life. There are, for example, many who feel, and that with some justice, that the New Testament is in a peculiar sense the sacred book of Christianity. Why, they ask, go to the Old Testament when we have the New with its more complete and perfect revelation? But this attitude reflects only a half truth, which is often more deceptive than an out and out falsehood. Certainly, Christians find their loftiest inspiration in the study of the life, character, and teaching of the Master and of his disciples; but the New Testament has by no means displaced the Old. The early Christians were right in placing it beside the New, because the former is still of inestimable value. Indeed, it is impossible to understand the New Testament properly unless one has an adequate knowledge of the Old. Moreover, there are many truths taken for granted in the New Testament for a biblical statement of which we must turn to the Old. Will the revelation of the nature and character of God contained in the Old Testament ever lose its doctrinal value? And even in cases where both Testaments cover the same field the Old retains a peculiar value. True, the New Testament presents a more complete and perfect revelation, but there are few New Testament truths which have not their roots in the Old. The former presents the full-grown revelation; nevertheless, a vast number of people, who have not yet reached a state of perfection, will understand even New Testament truths more readily as they are presented in the Old Testament; for here they can see the truths in more concrete form; they have flesh and blood; they are struggling for victory over darkness and superstition. Nearly all the great and vital doctrines of the Church, though founded principally on the New Testament, are illustrated, are made more real and human, become more impressive and forceful as we study their development and growth under the Old Testament dispensation.

The neglect of the Old Testament is due, in the second place, to a reaction against its misuse by former generations.([4]) Puritanism and the theology of the past three centuries were largely rooted in the Old Testament. From it the stern Puritans drew their spirit of justice, their zeal for righteousness, and their uncompromising condemnation of everything that appeared wrong. Their preachers nobly echoed the thunders of Sinai and the denunciations of Elijah and Amos; but in doing this they failed to recognize the divine love back of the prophetic message, and by their narrow interpretation of the letter, and their emphasis upon the more primitive and imperfect teaching of the Old Testament, they were often led to extremes that were neither biblical nor Christian. Against intolerance and persecution the human heart rebels, and with it comes a feeling of resentment against the cause. Thus it happened that the reaction against Puritanism brought with it a disregard of the Old Testament, which was followed either by the exaltation of the New Testament, whose spirit is more merciful and tender, or by hostility against the entire

Bible and Christianity as a whole. This abuse of the Old Testament was due in large part to the use of faulty, or erroneous, methods of interpretation. And since there seems to be even now a tendency in some places to defend these methods, which are out of keeping with the spirit of scientific investigation in this age, many intelligent men have come to look with suspicion upon a book in the study of which unscientific methods continue to be used.

Another important cause of the change of attitude toward the Old Testament is to be found in the labors expended upon the Old Testament by able scholars in the pursuit of a careful, critical study of the ancient records. As has been stated in another connection, these studies are not the outgrowth, as is often erroneously assumed, of a desire to discredit the Bible, to displace it from the heart and confidence of the people, or to attack its teaching or inspiration. "It would be a most hopeless thing," says W. G. Jordan, "to regard all this toil as the outcome of skepticism and vanity, a huge specimen of perverse ingenuity and misdirected effort."[5] They are simply the results of Protestantism and the Renaissance.[6] But whatever the spirit back of the study, and whatever the gains of this investigation, one result is that many Christians feel perplexed with regard to the true position of the Old Testament.

What of its claims? What of its inspiration? How far is it human in origin? How far divine? These and similar questions are asked by men everywhere. Never was there more interest, more inquiry, and, perhaps, more unrest and disquietude among thoughtful people.

Surely, it is high time to realize that all this investigation has had no harmful effect upon the substance of the divine revelations conveyed in the Old Testament records. In the words of Jordan, "To me, with my faith that the whole universe is filled with the presence of the living, self-revealing God, I cannot conceive . . . that the most severe criticism can ever banish the divine power from that great literature which is one of the choicest organs of its manifestations."[7] As has been pointed out in the preceding chapters, some long-cherished notions and interpretations have been overthrown; to some extent our ideas concerning its literary forms have had to be modified, but its substance has not been disturbed. On the contrary, it has come to be seen with a clearness unrecognized before that it bears the indelible stamp of God.

This being the case, students of the Bible should return to a more just appreciation of that part of Sacred Scripture which is so intimately connected with the training of Jesus and his disciples. If the Old Testament contains records and interpretations of divine revelations, those who claim to be children of God should be willing, yea, anxious, to put forth some efforts to familiarize themselves adequately with these records. But the sense of gratitude and appreciation for these self-revelations of God is not the only reason which should prompt the Christian to turn more frequently to the pages of the Old Book. A much more important consideration is the fact that the lessons taught in the Old Testament are of profound significance to-day, and that they cannot be neglected without serious consequences. Again, attention may be called to the fact that the Founder of Christianity and his disciples found nourishment in its pages, and that they constantly exhorted their followers to do the same. Now, Jesus is recognized by all Christians as a model worthy of imitation in every relation of life. Would it not be well to imitate him in the use of the Old Testament Scriptures? If he found in the pages of the Old Testament weapons with which to put to flight the Evil One, might not we?

Aside from these general considerations, it is easily shown that every part of the Old Testament is full of teaching which is of the highest value even in the twentieth century of the Christian era. Consider, for example, the first eleven chapters of Genesis, around which much controversy has raged. In former days these chapters were thought to give an absolutely accurate account of creation and the early history of mankind. However, various lines of investigation have shown this view to be untenable. "We are forced, therefore," says a recent writer, "to the conclusion that, though the writers to whom we owe the first eleven chapters of Genesis report faithfully what was currently believed among the Hebrews respecting the early history of mankind, yet there was much they did not know, and could not take cognizance of. These chapters, consequently, contain no account of the real beginnings, either of the earth itself, or of man and human civilization upon it."[8] All this need create not the slightest difficulty for one who holds the scriptural conception of the nature and purpose of the biblical writings. It is true of these chapters, as of other parts of the record, that "the only care of the prophetic tradition is to bring out clearly the religious origin of humanity."[9] If anyone is in search of accurate information regarding the age of this earth, or its relation to the sun, moon, or stars, or regarding the exact order in which plants and animals have appeared upon it, he should go to recent textbooks in astronomy, geology, and paleontology. It is not the purpose of the writers of Scripture to impart physical instruction, or to enlarge the bounds of scientific knowledge. So far as the

scientific or historical information imparted in
these chapters is concerned, it is of little more
value than the similar stories of other nations.
And yet the student of these chapters can see a
striking contrast between them and extra-biblical
stories describing the same unknown ages handed
down from pre-scientific centuries. Here comes
to view the uniqueness of the Bible. The other
traditions are of interest only as relics of a by-
gone past. Not so the biblical statements; they
are and ever will be of inestimable value, not
because of their scientific teaching, but because
of the presence of sublime religious truth in the
crude forms of primitive science. If anyone
wishes to know what connection the world has
with God, if he seeks to trace back all that now
is to the very fountain-head of life, if he desires
to discover some unifying principle, some illuminating purpose in the history of the earth, he may
turn to these chapters as his safest and, indeed,
only guide to the information he seeks.

The purpose of the narratives being primarily
religious, it is only natural that their lessons
should be religious lessons. The one supreme
lesson taught throughout the entire section is
"In the beginning, God." But each separate
narrative teaches its own peculiar lessons. The
more important of these are briefly summarized
by Driver as follows: "The narrative of creation

sets forth, in a series of dignified and impressive pictures, the sovereignty of God; his priority to and separation from all finite, material nature; his purpose to constitute an ordered cosmos, and gradually to adapt the earth to become the habitation of living beings; and his endowment of man with the peculiar, unique possession of self-conscious reason, in virtue of which he became capable of intellectual and moral life, and is even able to know and hold communion with his Maker. In chapters two and three we read, though, again, not in a historical but in a pictorial and symbolic form, how man was once innocent, how he became conscious of a moral law, and how temptation fell upon him and he broke that law. The fall of man, the great and terrible truth, which history not less than individual experience only too vividly teaches each one of us, is thus impressively set before us. Man, however, though punished by God, is not forsaken by him, nor left in his long conflict with evil without hope of victory. In chapter four the increasing power of sin, and the fatal consequence to which, if unchecked, it may lead, is vividly portrayed in the tragic figure of Cain. The spirit of vindictiveness and the brutal triumph in the power of the sword is personified in Lamech. In the narrative of the Flood God's wrath against sin and the divine prerogative of mercy are alike exemplified:

Noah is a standing illustration of the truth that 'righteousness delivereth from death,' and God's dealings with him after the Flood form a striking declaration of the purposes of grace and good will with which God regards mankind. The narrative of the Tower of Babel emphasizes Jehovah's supremacy in the world, and teaches how the self-exaltation of man is checked by God."( )

These chapters are followed by the stories of the patriarchs. Missionaries say—and experience at home has confirmed the claim—that the patriarchal narratives are of inestimable value to impress lessons of the reality and providence of God, and to encourage the exercise of faith and confidence in him. There is nothing that can be substituted for them in religious instruction. Lack of space will not permit to point out in detail the educational value of these documents; however, in passing, mention may be made of the fact that Professor W. W. White enumerates twenty-one Christian virtues that are illustrated and enforced in the life of Abraham.([11]) He was (1) steadfast, (2) resolute, (3) prudent, (4) tactful, (5) candid, (6) kind, (7) self-controlled, (8) obliging, (9) self-denying, (10) condescending, (11) unselfish, (12) peaceable, (13) hospitable, (14) courteous, (15) humble, (16) thankful, (17) reverent, (18) prayerful, (19) worshipful, (20) faith-

ful, (21) obedient. Not one iota of their value
for purposes of instruction in righteousness have
these records lost because doubt has been cast
upon their absolute historical accuracy. "Abraham is still the hero of righteousness and faith;
Lot and Laban, Sarah and Rebekah, Isaac, Jacob,
and Joseph, in their characters and experiences,
are still in different ways types of our own selves,
and still in one way or another exemplify the
ways in which God deals with the individual soul,
and the manner in which the individual soul
ought, or ought not, to respond to his leadings."[12]
What if some of these figures pass before us on
the stage rather than in real life, do they on that
account lose their vividness, their truthfulness,
their force ? " If," says J. E. McFadyen,[13] "it
should be made highly probable that the stories
were not strictly historical, what should we then
have to say? We should then have to say that
their religious value was still extremely high.
The religious truth to which they give vivid and
immortal expression would remain the same.
The story of Abraham would still illustrate the
trials and the rewards of faith. The story of
Jacob would still illustrate the power of sin to
haunt and determine a man's career, and the
power of God to humble, discipline, and purify
a self-confident nature. The story of Joseph
would still illustrate how fidelity amid tempta-

tion, wrong, and sorrow is crowned at last with glory and honor. The spiritual value of these and similar tales is not lost, even when their historical value is reduced to a minimum, for the truths which they illustrate are truths of universal experience." The present writer is convinced that even as historical documents these narratives are of immense value. Nevertheless, it may be well to remind ourselves again that the apostle does not point his readers to the Old Testament Scriptures for instruction in ancient history, but he claims that they are profitable "for teaching, for reproof, for correction, for instruction which is in righteousness"; and these records, whatever their historical shortcomings may be, are most assuredly profitable for all these purposes.

The historical books of the Old Testament are a continuous illustration of the reality of a Divine Providence, by revealing on almost every page the hand of God in human history. Only as we trace the history of the Hebrews can we understand the unfolding in the mind of man under the influence of the Divine Spirit of the great religious ideas and conceptions which have become the mainspring of human progress; the ideas which may be seen in crystallized form in modern Judaism, in perverted form in Mohammedanism, and in expanded and spiritualized form in Christianity. Preëminent among these conceptions is the idea of one personal holy and righteous God. The Hebrews were also the first to teach man that the supreme goal of life is righteousness, and thus they became the ethical teachers of the human race. They first gave objective expression to pure and lofty ethics in law. To-day the principles of Hebrew legislation are still the bone and marrow of the world's greatest legal systems. Though the Romans may be, to a large extent, responsible for the form which modern legal systems have adopted, the substance must be traced back to Hebrew legislation.

Moreover, the Hebrews prepared the way for Christianity. Jesus himself recognized that the faith he proclaimed was not a new creation. "Think not," said he, "that I came to destroy the law or the prophets: I came not to destroy, but to fulfill."([14]) He came to fill up, to spiritualize and intensify the religious and ethical teaching of the great leaders of the Hebrews. Men needed the preliminary training of the Old Testament dispensation before they were ready to appreciate the fuller revelation in and through Jesus the Christ, and Christianity could never have triumphed had it not been for the preparatory work of the religious and ethical teachers of the Hebrews, whose activity was very largely determined by the course of the nation's history. Again,

Jesus, according to the flesh, was a descendant of Abraham, reared in a Jewish home, and under Jewish influences. He studied Jewish literature and Jewish ideals were held up before him. All this must have made some impression upon the mind and life of the Master. He and his teaching can be understood only if he is studied in the light of Jewish thought and Jewish religion reaching back to the very beginning of Hebrew history. All this shows how important is the study of the historical books of the Old Testament to one who desires to appreciate fully the Christian religion.

It is impossible to estimate too highly the eternal value of the devotional literature of the Old Testament as illustrated, for example, in the book of Psalms. Well has it been said, "What the heart is in man, that is the Psalter in the Bible."[15] The Psalms touch the heart, because they are the expressions of the deepest feelings of the writers; and because these lyrics express personal experiences they may be, and are, used even to-day to express the various emotions of joy, sorrow, hope, fear, anticipation, etc., of persons who live even on a higher plane than did their authors. "What is there," says Richard Hooker,[16] "necessary for man to know which the Psalms are not able to teach? Heroical magnanimity, exquisite justice, grave moderation, exact wisdom, repentance unfeigned, unwearied patience, the mysteries of God, the sufferings of Christ, the terrors of wrath, the comforts of grace, the works of Providence over this world, and the promised joys of that world which is to come; all good, necessarily to be either known or done, or had, this one celestial fountain yieldeth; let there be any grief or disaster incident to the soul of man, any wound or sickness named for which there is not in this treasure-house a present comfortable remedy at all times ready to be found."

Manifold indeed are the contents of the Psalter; manifold the moods of the authors; and manifold the experiences they express. But there is one bond which unites them all into one living unity, namely, a sublime faith in Jehovah, the God of Israel. This variety on the one hand, and essential unity on the other, are the qualities which have given to the book in all ages a unique place in the religious life of the individual and of the Church of God. With full justice says Perowne:[17] "No single book of Scripture, not even the New Testament, has, perhaps, ever taken such hold on the heart of Christendom. None, if we dare judge, unless it be the Gospels, has had so large an influence in molding the affections, sustaining the hopes, purifying the faith of believers. With its words, rather than with their own, they have come before God. In these they have uttered their desires, their fears, their confessions, their aspirations, their sorrows, their joys, their thanksgivings. By these their devotion has been kindled and their hearts comforted. The Psalter has been in the truest sense the prayer book of both Jews and Christians."

Equally profitable is the study of the Wisdom literature. The wise men accepted the great religious truths proclaimed by the prophets; it was their business to apply them to the details of everyday life, and instruct their contemporaries in that application. They did an important and necessary work; they pointed out constantly and persistently that religion cannot be separated from the daily life. But the wise men were dealing with persons who had hardly gone beyond the childhood stage in things religious and ethical, hence they must put the most profound truths in the simplest possible form. They must abstain, as far as possible, from all speculation, and confine themselves to simple, practical precepts which would appeal to the ordinary practical common sense of the hearer. "The great desire of the sages," says Marshall, "was to reduce the lofty theistic morality which underlies Mosaism to brief, pithy sayings, easily remembered and readily applicable to the everyday life of man."[18] Certainly, in time they would be compelled to rise above simple precepts and try to solve some of the more perplexing problems of life; on the other hand, there would always be a demand for the more simple sayings of these moral guides. The Old Testament contains specimens of these different productions of wisdom activity. The book of Proverbs is a collection of the more simple, practical precepts, while the books of Job and Ecclesiastes illustrate speculative wisdom.

The charge has sometimes been made against the book of Proverbs that it is not truly religious, that it moves on a lower plane, and contemplates lower aims than the other books of the Old Testament; but this is only a half truth. That the book differs from other books is undoubtedly true, but that is due to the purpose of its author. He did not mean to collect prophetic discourses or sublime religious lyrics, but those simple precepts of life which, though simple, are ever needed for the proper conduct of man. There are two phases of religion: the one internal, the religious experience; the other external, the religious life. The two go together, though at times the one, at times the other, may be emphasized. The authors of the Proverbs emphasized chiefly the latter. They teach the most difficult of all lessons: how to practice religion; how to fulfill the duties and overcome the temptations of everyday life. But these wise men rested their practical teaching upon a religious basis. Their religion may not be on a New Testament level, but in this they resemble other Old Testament writings; their conceptions of reward and punishment may be crude, and at times materialistic, but this peculiarity they share with all those saints of Israel whose vision is limited to this world.

Underneath all their teaching there is a firm belief in the existence of a righteous God and the reality of his rule over the world, as also in the other great religious verities taught by the prophets. Far from disregarding religion, the writers of the Proverbs sought to make it the controlling motive of life and conduct. A profound religious spirit pervades the whole book; but in addition there are many passages which give definite expression to the lofty religious conceptions of the wise men.([19]) Nevertheless, as is natural in view of the purpose of the wise men, greater stress is laid upon ethics, the practice of religion. Nothing and no relation of life seems to have escaped the attention of the writers. Precepts are given concerning ordinary everyday conduct, the relations of men to their fellows, domestic relations and happiness, national life and the proper attitude toward the government, and other relations and interests of life. The permanent value of the book is suggested in these words of Davison:([20]) "For the writers of Proverbs religion means good sense, religion means mastery of affairs, religion means strength and manliness and success, religion means a well-furnished intellect employing the best means to accomplish the highest ends. There is a healthy, vigorous tone about this kind of teaching which is never out of date, but which, human nature being what it is, is only too apt to disappear in the actual presentation of religion in the Church on earth."

From simple practical precepts the wise men rose to speculation. Their speculative philosophy is theistic, for it starts from the conviction that there is a personal God. The best specimen of this type of Wisdom literature is the book of Job, which deals with the perplexing problem of evil and suffering. The book recounts how Job, a man of exemplary piety, was overtaken by an unprecedented series of calamities, and it reports the debate between Job and other speakers to which the occasion is supposed to have given rise. The experiences of the perfect Job raised the perplexing question, How can the suffering of a righteous man be harmonized with the belief in a holy and just God? The popular view, reflected in the greater portion of the Old Testament, was that suffering was always punishment for sin, prosperity reward for piety. Such belief seemed in accord with the righteousness of Jehovah. Undoubtedly, exceptions to the rule might be noted, but as long as the individual was looked upon simply as an atom in the national unit, the apparent inequalities in the fortunes of individuals would not constitute a pressing problem. When, however, especially through the teaching of Jeremiah and Ezekiel, the individual received proper recognition, an experience like that of Job was bound to create difficulties, for the suffering of a righteous man would seem to point to unfairness on the part of God. That this perplexity was felt is seen from allusions in the prophetic books. At last the time came when a wise man in Israel sought to solve the problem in the light of the religious knowledge he possessed.

The problem, then, discussed by the author of the book of Job is, How can the sufferings of a righteous man be harmonized with belief in a holy and righteous God? Various solutions of this problem are suggested in different parts of the book: (1) The solution of the prologue—Suffering is a test of character. (2) The solution of the friends—Suffering is always punishment for sin. (3) The solution of Job—Job struggles long and persistently with the problem; a few times he seems to have a glimpse of a possible straightening-out of the present inequalities after death, but it is only a glimpse; he always sinks back to a feeling of uncertainty and perplexity. His general attitude is that there must be something out of gear in the world, for the righteousness of God cannot be discerned as things are going now. (4) The solution of Elihu—Elihu agrees with the friends that suffering is closely connected with sin; but he emphasizes more than they the disciplinary purpose of suffering, which, he points out, is the voice of God warning men to return to Him. (5) The solution of Jehovah—The whole universe is an unfathomable mystery, in which the evil is no more perplexing than the good. In the presence of all mysteries the proper attitude is one of humble submission. (6) The solution of the epilogue—Returns to the opinion of the friends, for it teaches that righteousness will sooner or later be rewarded with prosperity even in this world.

It is chiefly in the solution of this age-long problem suggested by the author of the book of Job that the real value of the discussion lies. The author nowhere states which of the above-mentioned conclusions he accepts as true. As a result, he has been charged with raising a profound problem, discussing it with relentless logic, and then leaving it unsolved. This, however, is not quite fair to this ancient wise man. "With a touch too artistic to permit him to descend to a homiletic attitude, the poet has shown that his solution of life's problem is a religious one. He had portrayed with great power the inability of man's mind to comprehend the universe or to understand why man must suffer; but he makes Job, his hero, find in a vision of God the secret of life. Job's questions remain unanswered, but now that he knows God, he is content to let them remain unanswered. He cannot solve life's riddle, but is content to trust God, of whose goodness he is convinced, and who, Job is sure, knows the answer. The poet has thus taught that it is in the realm of religion, and not in that of the intellect, that the solution of life's mysteries is to be found."[21] Even Christianity has no other solution of the problem to offer; it must still insist upon a solution of faith, with a lofty conception of God, and a vision of life broad enough to include eternity, when the apparent inequalities of this life may be adjusted by a loving and righteous God.

The book of Ecclesiastes, dealing with the perplexities of life in general, full of pessimism and skepticism, is not without its permanent value. The author of the book has passed through many disappointments, and his spirit has grown somewhat skeptical and pessimistic. Everything has proved vanity: riches, pleasure, honor, even the search for wisdom; and he is not sure concerning his destiny after death. But over against his experiences in life there is a faith in God who governs the world. The book, which portrays the struggle between experience and faith, has aptly been called "a cry for light." The author does not see the light clearly, though here and there he may have a glimpse of it. The real perplexity is due to the fact that the author's horizon is bounded by the grave. In this life he sees no hope, therefore he looks with longing for a possible reckoning in an after life; but it remains a hope and cry, it never grows into a conviction. The more significant is the retention of his faith in God. He is conscious of a moral order in the world, though its operation is often frustrated; he is aware of cases in which the God-fearing man had an advantage over others. Hence, with all his uncertainty and doubt, he holds that it is his duty, and the duty of everyone else, to fear God and keep his commandments; God, somehow, will care for the mysteries and perplexities of life.

Even the Song of Songs, or Song of Solomon, often an object of ridicule, when rightly interpreted, is seen to bring suggestive lessons to the present age. The book owes its place in the canon of Sacred Scripture to the allegorical interpretation given to it from the earliest times. The Jews interpreted it as picturing the close relation existing between Jehovah and Israel; the Christians, as picturing the intimate fellowship between Christ and his bride, the Church. At present it is quite generally held that this interpretation does not do justice to the primary purpose of the book; but as to its original purpose two different views are held. According to both interpretations, the subject of the book is love—human love; the differences of opinion are with reference to the manner in which the subject is treated. Some think that the book is simply a collection of love or wedding songs, all independent of one another. Others feel that there are too many evidences of real unity in it to permit this interpretation; they see in the book a didactic drama or melodrama, the aim of the author being the glorification of true human love.

The drama centers around three principal characters—Solomon, the Shunammite maiden, and her shepherd lover. The book relates how the maiden, surprised by the king and his train, was brought to the palace in Jerusalem, where the king hoped to win her affections and to induce her to exchange her rustic home for the enjoyment and honor the court life affords. She has, however, already pledged her heart to a young shepherd; and the admiration and blandishments which the king lavishes upon her are powerless to make her forget him. In the end she is permitted to return to her mountain home, where at the close of the poem the lovers appear hand in hand and express, in warm, glowing words, the superiority of genuine spontaneous

affection. The real aim of the book, therefore,
seems to be to glorify true love, and more specifically, true betrothed love, which remains steadfast even in the most dangerous and most seductive
situations.

In this age, when the responsibility of the
individual Christian and of the Christian Church
toward the practical, social, religious, and moral
problems and evils is recognized more than at
any other previous time, the prophetic literature
is worthy of the most careful study on the part
of all Christians who recognize and who are
willing to meet their obligations to their day and
generation. The prophets of old met in the
strength of God, and at the divine impulse,
the problems and evils of their own age. They
had to face the problems of materialism and com-
mercialism; the evils resulting from the accumula-
tion of wealth, power, and resources in the hands
of a few; very serious economic problems; cruelty,
oppression, arrogance on the part of the rich pro-
prietors; corruption in government and in the
administration of justice; they had to grapple
with a cold, heartless formalism that threatened
to destroy pure, spiritual religion. Against these
evils and wrongs the prophets of old raised their
hands and voices. "When the old tribal customs
and bonds were weakened by the growth of cities
and the cultivation of commerce they saw that

society must be set upon a moral basis or suffer destruction. When the nation itself was about to be broken to pieces they saw in this a call for a deeper spiritual life. . . . They were interested in politics, but not as a profession in which to show their skill, or out of which they might gain wealth or glory. Politics for them meant simply the life of the nation in its relation to God and to the great outside world. They were social reformers. To the earlier prophets man was regarded always as a member of society rather than as an independent individual. . . . In opposition to a showy ritual, they set up their demands for justice between man and man."[22] Surely, it is a part of the Christian's duty to do his share toward a Christian solution of the social and religious problems of our day. We can hardly claim to have reached the full stature of Christian manhood or womanhood until we have acquired the knowledge and power to cope with these difficulties in the spirit of the Master and with the methods best adapted to the Christianizing of modern society. In these our efforts to lift humanity nearer to God, or to bring God nearer to humanity, we may learn much from the prophets of old.

To sum up the results of our study: As Christians we may find our loftiest inspiration in the study of the life, the character, and the teachings of the Master, and of the words of his disciples. But the New Testament is little more than a quarter of the Bible. In the preceding pages the attempt has been made to emphasize the permanent value of the larger division of the Sacred Book. It has been carefully scrutinized, tested in furnaces heated seven times, but out of the fire it has come bearing the stamp of God, testifying more confidently than ever before that God in olden times spake unto the fathers, and that in its pages may be found records and interpretations of these revelations. The features of the Old Testament which assure to it a permanent place in religious thought and life may be briefly indicated as follows:

The Old Testament will always prove attractive as literature. The more we know of other literatures of antiquity, the more evident it becomes that even from the literary viewpoint the Old Testament is far superior to any other literary remains of ancient civilization. "If the inimitable freshness of life is preserved in Homer, it is not less preserved in the epic stories of the Old Testament; while the still more intangible simplicity of the idyl is found perfect in Ruth and Tobit, the orations of Deuteronomy are as noble models as the orations of Cicero. Read by the side of the poetry of the Psalms, the lyrics of Pindar seem almost provincial. The imaginative poetry of

the Greeks is perfect in its own sphere, but by
the Hebrew prophets as bold an imagination is
carried into the mysteries of the spiritual world.
If the philosophy of Plato and his successors has
a special interest as the starting point for a progression of thought still going on as modern
science, yet the field of biblical wisdom offers an
attraction of a different kind, in a progression
of thought which has run its full round and has
reached a position of rest. . . . And in the inner
circle of the world's masterpieces, in which all
kinds of literary influences meet, the Bible has
placed Job, the Isaiahan Rhapsody, . . . unsur-
passed and unsurpassable."[23]

From the standpoint of history the Old Testament still occupies, and ever will occupy, a unique
position. Important as are the contributions of
archæology, the student of ancient history can
by no means spare the testimony of the Bible.
The Old Testament is still the main source of
information for the national history of the Hebrew people, and it is and will remain a very
important secondary source for the history of
the surrounding nations. It also retains a unique
place in the history of religion, for without it
the religious development of the Jews could
not be traced; and since the Jewish religion
is the foundation upon which Christianity was
developed, ignorance of that earlier religion

would prove a serious handicap to the student of Christianity.

The Old Testament will always be of value because of its intimate connection with the New. From the purely linguistic standpoint a knowledge of the former is essential for an understanding of the latter. New Testament modes of thought and expression are inexplicable without a study of the Old. There are many passages in the New Testament taken from the Old and referring back to it which cannot be properly understood unless we examine them in their original context. But the connection is even more vital, for in a very real sense the new dispensation has its roots in the old. It is one kingdom of God that is the subject of the history in both, and the Bible as a whole can never be rightly understood until the two Testaments are comprehended in their unity and harmony, for they are joined in inseparable unity in Christ himself.

Most important of all, the Old Testament retains, and ever will retain, a unique religious value. It will ever be important in the field of doctrine. True, the New Testament is the primary source for the doctrines of Christianity, but there are some things which the New Testament takes for granted, and for which we must turn to the Old. Will the revelation of the nature and character of God contained in the Old Testament ever lose its doctrinal value?—God, a spirit, personal, with a clearly defined moral character, in his mercy condescending to enter into covenant relations with his creatures, loving man and desiring to be loved by him, his anger aroused by sin, but gracious toward the repenting sinner? Again, have those early chapters of Genesis lost their doctrinal value? Has anyone supplied a substitute for the simple "In the beginning God created heaven and earth"?

The Old Testament is of permanent religious value because of its keen insight into human nature. The Bible has been called "the family album of the Holy God"; we might compare it, rather, to a picture gallery. What a variety! Everywhere we see them flesh and blood! Why is it they impress us so? Is it not because the pictures are so true to human nature that in spite of the difference in time, place, and circumstances they may serve even us as mirrors?

The Old Testament will always deserve study from the religious standpoint, because of the ideal of character it sets before us. "It presents to our souls characters that are supremely worthy of our reverence because consciously centered in God and full of his power. It permits us to share the enthusiasm of the men who discovered the fundamentals of our religion and the character of our God. It is indispensable to complete the

discipleship of Christ, because it is the creator
of the mold which his soul expanded."([24]) Its
types of character may lack the finer graces,
yet they are types we may do well to imitate.
Will the lives of Abraham, Joseph, Samuel, Elijah,
David, and many others ever lose their lessons?
What sublime ideals even the Christian minister
may find in the lives of the prophets!

Will we ever get beyond the moral duties which
are, according to the Old Testament, obligatory
upon man? Purity of thought, sincerity of motive, singleness of purpose, truthfulness, honesty,
justice, generosity, love—these are some of the
virtues which again and again are in the strong-
est language insisted upon in the pages of the
Old Book. Indeed, the Old Testament emphasizes the loftiest ideals of human life and society,
anticipating the time when in all the world the
universal Fatherhood of God and the common
brotherhood of man would be realized. In an
editorial in the Expository Times, commenting
upon a paper read before the First International
Moral Education Congress, are found these suggestive words: "It is when the teaching of the
Old Testament is simple, frank, and historical
that it becomes the best text-book of ethics in
the world, for it possesses these two incomparable
advantages—it is full of humanity, and it is full
of variety. The epics of Joseph and David, the

tragedies of Elijah and Isaiah have an undying charm. And the examples are varied as they are interesting. It offers examples of almost every stage of moral development. Whatever the pupil's moral attitude, there is some Jewish hero that appeals to him. That hero's actions can be traced to their motives and followed to their consequences. He can be treated with sympathy in so far as he attains the standard of his times, and yet criticized in so far as his motives are not those which we recognize as absolute. So the pupil may learn at once to appropriate those *media axiomata* which fit him, and yet realize that there is something beyond and above them."[25]

The Old Testament is of permanent significance because of its insistence on pure and spiritual religion, and its condemnation of all cold and external formalism. These words of the prophet Isaiah imply a lofty conception of true religion: "What unto me is the multitude of your sacrifices? saith Jehovah: I have had enough of the burnt-offerings of rams, and the fat of fed beasts; and I delight not in the blood of bullocks, or of lambs, or of he-goats. When ye come to appear before me, who hath required this at your hand, to trample my courts? Bring no more vain oblations; incense is an abomination unto me; new moon and sabbath, the calling of assemblies

—I cannot away with iniquity and the solemn meeting. Your new moons and your appointed feasts my soul hateth; they are a trouble unto me; I am weary of bearing them. And when ye spread forth your hands, I will hide mine eyes from you; yea, when ye make many prayers, I will not hear: your hands are full of blood. Wash you, make you clean; put away the evil of your doings from before mine eyes; cease to do evil; learn to do well; seek justice, relieve the oppressed, judge the fatherless, plead for the widow."[26] And the prophetic definition of religion, "He hath showed thee, O man, what is good; and what doth Jehovah require of thee, but to do justly, and to love kindness, and to walk humbly with thy God?"[27] is in no wise inferior to that given in the New Testament: "Pure religion and undefiled before our God and Father is this, to visit the fatherless and widows in their affliction, and to keep oneself unspotted from the world."[28]

Finally, how can we estimate highly enough the devotional value of the Old Testament as illustrated, for example, in the book of Psalms? Here we have the outpourings of human souls in the closest fellowship with their God, giving without restraint expression to the most various emotions, hopes, desires, and aspirations. What other literary compositions lift us into such atmosphere of religious thought and emotion?

Surely, the sweet singers enjoy a preëminence from which they can never be dethroned.

It is quite safe, therefore, to assert, that as long as human nature is what it is now the Old Testament must remain an ever-flowing fountain of living truth, able to invigorate and to restore, to purify and to refine, to ennoble and to enrich the moral and spiritual being of man. "No man," says A. W. Vernon,([29]) "save Jesus, ever had the right to lay the Book . . . aside, and he made it immortal."

NOTES ON CHAPTER VI

([1]) J. C. Todd, Politics and Religion in Ancient Israel, p. vii.

([2]) The Origin and Permanent Value of the Old Testament, p. 7.

([3]) Contemporary Review, August, 1889, p.232.

([4]) C. F. Kent, The Origin and Permanent Value of the Old Testament, pp. 5ff.

([5]) Biblical Criticism and Modern Thought, p. 6.

([6]) See above, p. 79.

([7]) Biblical Criticism and Modern Thought, p. 230.

([8]) S. R. Driver, The Book of Genesis, p. xlii.

([9]) A. Westphal, The Law and the Prophets, p. 43.

([10]) S. R. Driver, The Book of Genesis, p. lxx.

([11]) W. W. White, Studies in Old Testament Characters, p. 14.

([12]) S. R. Driver, The Book of Genesis, p. lxviii.

([13]) Old Testament Criticism and the Christian Church, p. 335.

([14]) Matt. 5. 17.

([15]) These words of Johannes Arnd are used by Franz

Delitzsch as the motto for his Commentary on the Psalms.

([16]) Ecclesiastical Polity, Book V, Chapter XXXVII, 2.

([17]) The Book of Psalms, Vol. I, p. 18.

([18]) J. T. Marshall, Job and His Comforters, p. 4.

([19]) For example, 3. 5–7; 16. 3, 6, 9; 23. 17.

([20]) W. T. Davison, The Wisdom Literature of the Old Testament, pp. 134, 135.

([21]) G. A. Barton, The Book of Job, p. 12.

([22]) W. G. Jordan, Biblical Criticism and Modern Thought, pp. 284, 285.

([23]) Richard G. Moulton, The Modern Reader's Bible, One Vol. ed., p. x.

([24]) A. W. Vernon, The Religious Value of the Old Testament, p. 80.

([25]) Expository Times, November, 1908, pp. 54, 55.

([26]) Isa. 1. 11–17.

([27]) Mic. 6. 8.

([28]) James 1. 27.

([29]) The Religious Value of the Old Testament, p. 81

INDEX

Abraham, 238.
Adad-nirari IV, 134.
Ahab, 131ff.
Angels, 182f.
Animism, 165f., 169f.
Appeal to the soul, 30ff.
Archæological material, 123f.
Archæology, 110ff.
Ashurbanipal, 140.
Assumption versus knowledge, 217ff.
Authorship, of Pentateuch, 88f.; other books, 89f.

Babylon, fall of, 141.
Benefits of criticism, 105ff.
Bible and Reason, 33f.
Bible lands, 111.
Black Obelisk, 133f.

Canon, 86f.
Ceremonial system, 178ff.
Character study, 238, 258f.
Christian consciousness, 36.
Comparative religion, 160ff.
Comparative study, 160ff.; aim, 160; attitude toward, 161f.; importance, 164
Compilation, 87f.
Composition, 21–23.
Confirmations, 156.

Conflict between science and Genesis, 41ff.
Contrasts, 221f.
Cosmology of appearances, 59f.
Creation, 41ff.; story of, 201ff.; permanent value, 235f.
Criticism, 66ff.; benefits, 105ff.; definition, 67f.; Jesus and c., 92ff.; inspiration and c., 98ff., 105.
Cyrus, 141.

David, 104.
Day of Creation, 45f.
Decalogue, 199, 214ff.
Deity, conception of, 165ff., 206f., 212; Babylonian, 165–169, Egyptian, 169, Hebrew, 169–172; Character of D., 173ff.
Demons, 183f.
Devotional literature, 17f., 242f.
Divine element, 26ff.
Doctrinal value, 257f.

Ecclesiastes, 250f.
Elephantine, 141.
Eponym lists, 153.